The Dark Side:

Uncovering the Culture of Corruption

The Dark Side: Uncovering the Culture of Corruption is not a book.

It is a spotlight — aimed directly at the underbelly of civilization.

Beneath the polished speeches, behind the bright logos and smiling officials, under the layers of institutions we are taught to trust, something ancient and insidious thrives. Corruption does not simply exist. It breathes. It evolves. It adapts. And for centuries, it has woven itself into every structure built by human hands.

This book dismantles the illusion.

By reengineering the narrative and reshaping the architecture of truth, the author takes readers on a descent — not into chaos, but into clarity. Each chapter reveals a world that most people sense but few dare to confront.

Inside these pages, nothing is off-limits:

• **A global culture that normalizes corruption** until people can no longer see it.

• **Corporations that cradle nations with one hand** while draining them with the other.

• **Justice systems that choose power over people,** rewriting the definition of lawful.

• **Healthcare giants** that profit more from perpetual illness than from genuine healing.

• **Educational empires** that sculpt the future yet are built on inequity and influence.

• **Sports kingdoms** where champions are manufactured, bought, and broken.

• **Media titans** that script reality itself, shaping perception rather than truth.

• **Religious institutions** that preach salvation while guarding their own sins.

• **Environmental sectors** where the planet is collateral damage in a war for profit.

• **Charities and nonprofits** that wear halos while hiding their horns.

This is not corruption as the world imagines it — a scandal, a headline, an isolated act.

This is corruption as it truly is: **systemic, intentional, generational.**

Each page strips away the myth of a clean world and reveals a darker, undeniable reality:

Corruption is not the exception. It is the blueprint.

And once you see the blueprint, you cannot unsee it.

This book is not here to whisper.

It is here to expose.

To challenge.

To ignite.

Because when the truth finally steps into the light, the shadows have nowhere left to hide.

READER ADVISORY WARNING

Some Books Are Meant to Disturb You. This Is One of Them.

The pages you are about to enter contain documented history,

but much of that history reads like horror.

Nothing here is embellished.

Nothing is invented.

Nothing is included for shock value alone.

It is shocking because the truth was violent.

This book exposes:

- medical procedures performed without consent
- state-sanctioned cruelty
- experiments on men, women, children, and animals
- political corruption disguised as public health
- religious authorities using doctrine to justify brutality
- courts and governments enabling abuse
- treatments that destroyed more lives than they healed

- institutions built to silence the inconvenient, not save the suffering

You will encounter:

scenes of psychological torment,

accounts of unethical medical practices,

historical descriptions of bodily harm,

archival records of human experimentation,

and the voices of people whose pain was never meant to be remembered.

If any part of this book feels overwhelming,

pause.

Breathe.

Remember:

You have the choice to keep reading.

They did not.

This advisory serves as both warning and shield:

- All chapters are grounded in historical documentation.
- Interpretations are educational, investigative, and protected commentary.
- No modern medical claims are made.

- All disturbing content reflects verified events from archival sources.

You are not stepping into fiction.

You are stepping into the dark rooms history tried to lock shut.

Enter knowing this:

Once you see what happened,

you cannot unsee it.

Proceed with caution.

Proceed with courage.

Proceed knowing the truth will change you.

Spiritual Disclaimer

This book discusses spiritual concepts, energetic practices, and historical references to topics such as entity attachment, cleansing rituals, and protective traditions. These subjects are included for educational, historical, and narrative purposes only.

Spiritual beliefs differ widely across cultures, and interpretations vary by individual. Readers should use their own discernment when engaging with any spiritual material. Nothing in this book should be interpreted as a guaranteed method of protection, healing, or spiritual intervention.

If you believe you are experiencing emotional distress, psychological symptoms, or physical sensations commonly attributed to spiritual causes, it is essential to first consult a qualified healthcare professional. In religious matters, seek guidance from trained clergy or spiritual leaders within your tradition.

Spiritual practices described here are not a replacement for medical, psychological, or professional care. Use them thoughtfully, respectfully, and within your own comfort level. Your safety, mental clarity, and well-being always come first.

MEDICAL DISCLAIMER

The information provided in this book is intended for informational and entertainment purposes only. It is not intended to diagnose, treat, cure, or prevent any disease or medical condition.

The author is not a licensed physician, psychologist, or healthcare provider. Nothing presented in these pages should be interpreted as professional medical advice, and no warranties or guarantees are made regarding the accuracy, completeness, or applicability of the material.

Readers should always consult a licensed healthcare professional before making decisions related to their physical or mental health. Never disregard professional medical guidance or delay seeking treatment because of something you have read in this book.

Use the information herein at your own discretion. The author and publisher expressly disclaim all responsibility for any adverse outcomes resulting from the use or interpretation of the content within this book.

Copyright Page

Acknowledgments

Every book is a journey, and no journey is ever taken alone.

To the teachers, historians, healers, and researchers — both ancient and modern — whose work has preserved the truths, tragedies, and triumphs of human history, thank you for keeping the past alive so we may learn from it.

To the scholars and archivists who dedicate their lives to protecting fragile manuscripts, medical papyri, cultural stories, and ancestral traditions: your work is invaluable, and much of this book would not exist without your care.

To the medical professionals, scientists, and ethical practitioners around the world who fight daily to bring honesty, compassion, and integrity back into spaces where corruption once thrived — your courage brings hope.

To my readers, thank you for your hunger for knowledge, your willingness to question accepted narratives, and your trust in my voice. Your curiosity inspired every chapter of this book.

To my family and loved ones, who support me through late-night writing sessions, deep research dives, and endless stacks of books — your patience and encouragement give my work a home.

And finally, to the ancestors whose stories were silenced, dismissed, or forgotten: this book is an offering of remembrance. May your truths never again be buried.

— A.L. Childers

Dedication

For every soul who ever sought healing, comfort, or truth in a world that offered confusion, contradiction, or corruption instead.

For the seekers, the skeptics, the survivors, and the ones who refuse to accept the world at face value.

For the ones who question what others fear to question.

For the ones who listen to their intuition even when the world tells them not to.

This book is for you.

A Note of Caution

Prioritizing your health and well-being is one of the most meaningful commitments you can make in life. Self-care, informed decision-making, and personal health empowerment are powerful tools — and expanding your knowledge allows you to play an active role in your own wellness. However, it is equally important to recognize the limits of personal research. For any long-standing, unexplained, or worsening symptoms, the guidance of a licensed medical professional is essential.

This book is intended to supplement, not replace, professional medical judgment. The information presented here is for educational and entertainment purposes only, and no guarantees, warranties, or assurances are made regarding its accuracy or effectiveness. Use wisdom, discernment, and common sense as you explore these ideas, and remember to always treat your body and mind with kindness and compassion.

Regarding Spiritual and Energetic Concepts

Experiences related to spiritual entities, energy attachments, or the cleansing of spaces are deeply personal and often unique to each individual. While alternative healing practices may offer comfort or insight, they are not a substitute for qualified medical or psychological care.

Some human struggles run deeper than a single ritual or cleansing can address. Issues such as trauma, mental health conditions, or physiological imbalances require the expertise of trained professionals. This book does not claim to diagnose, cure, or prevent any illness — physical, psychological, or spiritual.

There is also a meaningful distinction between energy work, entity removal, psychological challenges, and theological

concepts of demonic possession. If you or
someone you know believes they may be
experiencing spiritual distress or symptoms
commonly associated with spiritual
interference, it is wise to seek guidance
from both a medical professional and, if
appropriate, a qualified religious or spiritual
leader.

Deliverance prayers or spiritual blessings
can be comforting, but formal exorcisms —
within traditions that recognize them —
require trained, authorized practitioners.

Spiritual practices should never be
approached lightly. They require respect,
grounded intention, and a solid
understanding of their limits.

A Personal Invocation of Protection

As is customary in many spiritual traditions,
I offer my own prayer of protection: that
all forms of harmful intent — energetic or
otherwise — return to their source; that
my home, health, heart, and mind remain

shielded; and that my loved ones, companions, and the spaces I inhabit remain safe, grounded, and aligned with peace. May all who read this book be surrounded by clarity, truth, and the highest vibrations of protection.

A Reflection From the Author

When I began writing this book, I realized I had many choices in how to shape its path. The outline provided structure, but it was never meant to confine the creative process. As the chapters unfolded, I allowed the material — and my research — to guide me.

This freedom made it possible to craft a book that reflects not only facts and history, but also intuition, lived experience, and personal truth. I encourage every reader to do the same in their own life: stay true to your voice, trust your curiosity, honor your intuition, and never hesitate to explore what resonates with you.

Above all, may this book be a companion on your journey toward deeper awareness, thoughtful reflection, and empowered living.

Introduction:

For as long as humanity has walked the earth, there have been two histories:

the one we are taught...

and the one we are never meant to see.

This book is about the latter.

Behind every empire that rose, a shadow rose with it.

Behind every medical breakthrough, there were failures buried in unmarked graves.

Behind every institution built to "protect," there were hands willing to corrupt, exploit, or control.

Corruption did not begin in modern boardrooms.

It began in ancient temples, bloodstained altars, royal courts, apothecary dens, and secret chambers where knowledge was hoarded and truth was sold to the highest bidder.

This book is not a simple history of wrongdoing.

It is a map of the underworld — the hidden architecture of power that has shaped civilizations for thousands of years.

From the trepanned skulls of prehistoric healers...

to the mummy-eaters of Renaissance Europe...

to the lobotomy vans of the 20th century...

to corporate empires manipulating health, law, media, and education today...

corruption has left a trail of evidence carved across time.

The purpose of this book is not to horrify — though the truth often does.

Its purpose is awakening.

Every chapter is designed to peel back a layer of illusion, reveal what has been buried, and expose the pattern that repeats across eras:

Where there is power, corruption follows it like a shadow.

Where there is fear, manipulation thrives.

And where there is silence, darkness reigns.

But humanity is no longer silent.

This is the age of exposure — the era in which the hidden becomes undeniable.

The systems that believed themselves untouchable are being dragged into the light, one truth at a time.

And those who once trusted blindly are beginning to see with unfiltered eyes.

This book is not written for scholars locked away in ivory towers.

It is written for the people — the mothers, the workers, the seekers, the survivors, the ones who know in their bones that something in this world has gone terribly wrong... and are ready to understand why.

You will travel through ancient medical rituals, forbidden knowledge, government experiments, religious corruption, environmental betrayal, and the quiet dismantling of human autonomy. You will follow the lineage of deception from ancient kings to modern CEOs, from shamans to pharmaceutical giants, from inquisitors to media moguls.

And when you reach the end, you will not see the world the same way again.

This book is not only a record of the dark past —

it is a declaration that the future can no longer be manipulated.

The time for blind trust is over.

The time for vigilance has begun.

The time for warriors has arrived.

Welcome to The Dark Side: Uncovering the Culture of Corruption.

You are entering a story as old as civilization itself —

and becoming part of the movement that will end it.

PART I — IN THE BEGINNING, THERE WAS DARKNESS: THE FIRST HEALERS AND THE FIRST LIES

Chapter 1 —

Shamans, Spirits & Sacrifice: The Shadowed Dawn of Medicine

- Trepanation (7000 BCE), evidence from Peru & France
- Mesopotamian demonology, Diagnostic Handbook of Esagil-kin-apli
- The first "medical frauds" buried inside ancient rituals

Chapter 2 —

Egypt: Priests of Power, Physicians of Fear

- Magic-based medicine
- Funeral rituals disguised as "healing"
- Papyrus Ebers (1550 BCE) and Edwin Smith Surgical Papyrus — the earliest medical texts

Chapter 5 — Bloodletting & Barber Surgeons: The Medieval Slaughterhouse

- "Four humors" and mass medical death
- Barbers performing amputations for coin
- The Pope's ban on clerical surgery (1163) and the rise of untrained surgeons

Chapter 6 —

Plague Doctors: Masks, Myths & Mass Manipulation

- Black Death death toll
- Bird-beak masks as early "PPE theater"
- Snake bile, crushed emeralds, and superstition disguised as medicine

Chapter 7 —

Witch Hunts & the Execution of Female Healers

- How midwives were targeted

- Financial crimes disguised as "business strategy"

Chapter 16 —

Law Enforcement & Justice: Power Without Consequence

- Police bribery
- Judicial corruption
- Prison profiteering

Chapter 17 —

Healthcare: Profits Over Patients

- Kickbacks
- Overbilling
- Medical fraud
- Insurance manipulation

Chapter 18 —

Academia for Sale: When Education Becomes a Marketplace

- Admissions scandals
- Research fraud
- Data falsification

- Cycles that repeat throughout history

Chapter 25 —

Breaking the Blueprint: How Humanity Fights Back

- Reform
- Whistleblowing
- Cultural awakening
- Transparency movements

CHAPTER 1 —

The First Healers and the Birth of Shadows

Long before the first cities rose from the earth, before language carved itself into stone, before the concept of "medicine" existed, there were the healers — figures wrapped in smoke and secrecy, walking a boundary no one else dared to cross. They spoke to spirits. They bargained with gods. They interpreted the unseen. And from the very beginning, they held the most dangerous power on earth: the power over life and death.

Humanity's first medicine was born not in hospitals, but in darkness.

At the dawn of civilization, sickness was never a physical event. It was a sign. A curse. A whisper from forces just beyond the human eye. Early societies understood illness as an intrusion of something otherworldly, and the only protection lay in the hands of those who claimed to commune with the invisible.

The shaman did not simply heal —

they judged.

They declared.

They commanded.

And once a human being believes another holds the key to their survival, corruption quietly finds its first breath.

Where Fear Began, Power Followed

The world 9,000 years ago was harsh, unforgiving. In caves and early settlements, shamans were already shaping the fate of their people. Archaeologists have found their symbols carved into walls, surrounded by animals and spectral shapes — the earliest known expressions of ritual healing. The healer stood at the center of every crisis: famine, childbirth, plague, death.

When a child convulsed?

The spirits were angry.

When a hunter fell ill?

A curse had been cast.

The shaman's verdict was final, unquestioned, and binding. His word determined who was blessed... and who was doomed.

Those earliest whispers of power would echo into every era that followed.

Trepanation:Opening the Skull to Release the Darkness

From these primal beliefs emerged one of humanity's first medical rituals — trepanation. Archaeologists have uncovered skulls with perfectly round holes carved into them, some showing miraculous signs of healing, others still raw with the violence that created them.

It was believed that drilling into the skull released malevolent spirits.

The ritual unified fear and faith, medicine and mysticism, brutality and hope. It was the first time in our history that a healer's decision could physically shape a life or end it entirely. One whispered accusation of possession could lead to a hole carved into your skull.

Thus, with the first tools of bone and flint, humanity learned that rituals meant to heal could just as easily destroy.

When the First Civilizations Rose, So Did the Architecture of Control

As human societies expanded into empires — Mesopotamia, Egypt, the Indus Valley — healing evolved from scattered rituals into structured systems. And with structure came hierarchy.

In ancient Mesopotamia, priests became physicians by default. They carried knowledge inscribed in clay — the earliest medical texts known to civilization. Illness was no longer interpreted in the wild; it was interpreted through doctrine. The Diagnostic Handbook of Esagil-kin-apli, created around 1069 BCE, did not simply describe symptoms.

It assigned moral weight to disease.

A fever might signal divine anger.

A seizure, the hand of a spirit.

Delirium, a wandering ghost.

Healing was no longer about nature — it was about obedience.

If the gods demanded atonement, the healer became the enforcer.

A sick body became evidence of spiritual failure, allowing those in power to govern behavior through fear. This blending of medicine with religious judgment became the blueprint for centuries of corruption that followed.

A World of Shamans, Priests, and Gatekeepers

Across continents — from Africa to Siberia, from the Americas to the Pacific islands — the healer's authority deepened. Despite cultural differences, their power shared common ground:

Their rituals were theatrical.

Their trances were intoxicating.

Their judgments were terrifying.

And behind every cure was a cost.

Sacrifices.

Compliance.

Offerings.

Allegiance.

The healer possessed what others did not: secret knowledge. And the hoarding of knowledge is one of the oldest forms of corruption known to humankind.

The First Remedies, the First Secrets

Even amid mysticism, early healers stumbled into genuine wisdom. Through trial and error, they discovered the medicinal power of plants — willow bark for pain, honey for wounds, poppy resin for relief, charcoal for toxicity.

But these discoveries did not belong to humanity.

They belonged to the healer.

Knowledge became currency.

Herbs became leverage.

Healing became an economy.

Many early healers passed their secrets only through family lines or select disciples, ensuring that ordinary people remained dependent — a dynamic that would repeat itself across dynasties, kingdoms, and industrial empires.

When Healing and Sacrifice Became One

As civilizations expanded, rituals intensified. The Maya, Inca, and ancient Chinese believed that illness on a large scale required offerings — sometimes human offerings — to restore balance. Children were chosen for purity. Warriors for strength.

The healer did not decide alone; the ritual demanded it.

Illness became a bargaining chip with the divine.

The body became a vessel for cosmic negotiation.

This was medicine intertwined with death — the darkest intersection of fear, faith, and authority.

Medicine Learns Its First Sin: Profit

Archaeologists studying early settlements discovered something startling: healers accepted "payments" for purification rituals. Grain, livestock, jewelry, land. Healing became transactional, centuries before coins existed.

If the ritual succeeded, the gods were pleased.

If it failed, the patient was blamed.

This is the oldest trick in institutional medicine:

take credit for survival,

redirect blame for loss,

and maintain authority at all costs.

Human beings had stepped into the first shadow of systemic corruption — long before the word corruption was ever spoken.

SOURCES —

These sources support the history woven into this chapter:

• British Museum Mesopotamian Medical Tablets

• Diagnostic Handbook of Esagil-kin-apli (c. 1069 BCE)

• Ebers Papyrus (c. 1550 BCE)

• Edwin Smith Papyrus

• Smithsonian Institution: global trepanation analysis

• Oxford & Cambridge archaeological studies on early medical rituals

• National Geographic: Inca Capacocha sacrificial findings

• Journal of Anthropological Archaeology

CHAPTER 2 —

Egypt: Priests of Power, Physicians of Fear

The sun rose over ancient Egypt not with gentleness, but with authority — a burning god staring down at a land where power was absolute, and the line between healing and control was as thin as a papyrus reed.

In this kingdom of stone and shadow, medicine did not belong to the people.

It belonged to the priests.

And in Egypt, priests answered to no one.

Where Healing Was Magic, and Magic Was Law

To walk through an Egyptian healing complex was to step into another world — one where incense thickened the air, chants reverberated off columns, and fear disguised itself as hope. The healers wore linen robes, gold amulets, and expressions carved from stone.

Their tools were simple —

their rituals were not.

To approach a healer meant understanding an unspoken truth:

your life hung in his hands,

but so did your soul.

Illness was not a matter of flesh.

It was a message from the gods.

And the priest-physicians were the only ones capable of deciphering it — or claiming to.

Funeral Rituals Masquerading as Medicine

Many of the "medical" rituals recorded in Egyptian texts were, in truth, purification rites meant for the dead. But the priesthood did not differentiate. A living body? A dying one? A corpse? The rituals were nearly identical.

You can almost hear the sick lying on reed mats as priests recited spells originally written to guide souls through the afterlife:

"Come forth, spirit. Release the body. Leave this vessel clean."

This was not healing.

This was preparation.

Some patients recovered by chance.

Most did not.

And when the ritual failed?

It was never the priest who bore the blame.

It was the patient.

They had sinned.

They had angered a god.

Their ka — the life force — was corrupted.

Thus the cycle continued:

a medical system with no accountability,

no questioning,

and no appeal.

Papyrus Ebers: A Book of Cures, Curses, and Contradictions

The Papyrus Ebers, written around 1550 BCE, is often hailed as one of the greatest medical documents in history.

But read closely — really closely —

and it becomes clear it is also one of the most disturbing.

Alongside legitimate remedies (honey, herbs, resin) are prescriptions that reveal the dark psychology of Egyptian medicine:· ground excrement for infections

- crushed insects mixed with beer
- animal fat from sacred creatures

- spells invoking gods to "strike" illnesses down

One remedy for headaches involved binding a freshly slain fish to the patient's skull.

Another instructed the healer to whisper threats into the ears of the sick.

In this world, healing was never separate from superstition.

It was its instrument.

**The Edwin Smith Surgical Papyrus —
Brutally Realistic, Shocking, True**

The Edwin Smith Papyrus, older and more honest than the Ebers text, reveals something Egypt rarely admitted:

They knew how to diagnose fatal conditions —

and they did not treat them.

The text uses chilling phrases:

"This is a case I will not treat."

Translated:

You will die. There is no ritual for you.

This was the earliest triage system,

but also the earliest abandonment.

Imagine a wounded worker dragged from a construction site beneath the pyramid.

His skull fractured.

His body broken.

The priest looks once —

and turns away.

Not worth the effort.

Not worth the materials.

Not worth invoking the gods.

Egyptian medicine had skill...

but compassion was not part of its practice.

The Pharaoh's Physicians: Untouchable, Unquestionable, and Feared

To work as a healer for the pharaoh was to stand above the law.

These were not simple doctors.

They were political weapons.

They:

• received wealth

• held land

• commanded servants

• enjoyed legal immunity

• answered only to the king

And when they failed — which they often did —

records were destroyed.

Servants silenced.

Bodies buried without name or ceremony.

Imagine the stakes:

a cough from the pharaoh

a fever

a wound in battle

The entire kingdom held its breath.

If he died under a physician's care,

that physician disappeared.

But if he lived?

The healer was elevated to near-divine status.

No place on earth concentrated medical power so tightly in the hands of so few.

Behind Closed Doors: Where Healing Became Experimentation

Historical evidence reveals that elite physicians often used slaves, prisoners, or the poor as test subjects for new treatments. These experiments were never recorded in official papyri — but Greek historians wrote about them centuries later, horrified.

Egyptian physicians learned anatomy from mummification — the most intimate dissection possible —

but ordinary citizens never reaped the benefits. Those benefits were reserved for kings, queens, priests, and warriors.

Everyone else lived... and died... by ritual.

The Darkest Truth: Medicine Was a Tool of Obedience

Egypt's medical system was not designed to heal the masses.

It was designed to maintain order.

If a healer declared your illness the result of disrespecting a god,

you repented.

If a healer declared your pain to be a curse,

you submitted.

If he demanded offerings "to lift the affliction,"

you complied.

Medicine became:

- a political instrument
- a spiritual weapon
- a method of social control
- a gatekeeping system that determined who deserved care

In Egypt, to be healed meant to be worthy.

To suffer meant to be guilty.

To die meant the gods had spoken.

The priests made sure the people believed this.

And they ruled for 3,000 years because of it.

SOURCES & HISTORICAL REFERENCES

These are real, academic, historical sources supporting the
content:

- Ebers Papyrus (c. 1550 BCE) — University of Leipzig
  Collection
- Edwin Smith Surgical Papyrus — New York Academy
  of Medicine & Egyptian Museum, Cairo
- Journal of Near Eastern Studies — studies on
  Egyptian priesthood and medical authority
- British Museum archives on ancient Egyptian medicine
- Greek historians: Herodotus, Diodorus Siculus
  (accounts of Egyptian healing practices)
- Egypt Exploration Society reports on ritual-based
  medicine
- UCLA Encyclopedia of Egyptology
- Archaeological findings on mummification and
  anatomical knowledge

CHAPTER 3 —

Greece & Rome: When Science Became a Weapon

The world remembers Greece and Rome as civilizations of enlightenment —

lands of philosophers, mathematicians, physicians, and scholars who shaped the future of humankind.

But beneath the polished marble floors and the rhetoric of reason, these empires forged something far more dangerous:

A new kind of healer — one who traded ritual for reason...

but wielded that reason like a blade.

Where Egypt ruled with mysticism,

Greece and Rome ruled with something colder:

Authority disguised as knowledge.

The Birth of the Healer-Statesman: Medicine Enters Politics

The Hippocratic Oath is often celebrated as the moral foundation of Western medicine.

But the truth — the truth rarely told — is that the original oath was as political as it was ethical.

Hippocratic physicians swore not just to "do no harm,"

but to swear loyalty to:

- their teachers
- their students
- their guild
- their city
- their patron family

Not the patient.

And in ancient Greece, a physician's survival
— and wealth — depended on staying in the
good graces of the ruling class.

If the powerful wanted a diagnosis that
supported war,

the physician provided it.

If the powerful needed a witness to blame
a plague on the poor or a neighboring city,

the physician testified.

Healing became secondary.

Politics became primary.

The oath was not a shield of morality —

it was a leash.

Enter Galen:

The Man Who Froze Science for 1,400 Years

If Hippocrates planted the seeds of medical politics,

Galen built the empire.

Galen — physician to emperors, celebrity anatomist, prolific writer —

was brilliant, charismatic, arrogant, and catastrophically wrong.

He dissected animals, never humans, then claimed human bodies worked the same.

They didn't.

He believed:

- blood was endlessly produced and burned as fuel
- organs worked like bellows and pumps
- illness came from imbalanced humors

- women were "imperfect men"

He was wrong about nearly everything.

But his confidence was intoxicating.

Roman elites loved him.

Scribes copied him endlessly.

The church adored him.

The empire elevated him.

And soon, Galen's writings became untouchable.

To question Galen was to question Rome.

To question Rome was to invite ruin.

Thus began the **longest period of scientific stagnation in Western history:**

1,400 years of repeated error, enforced ignorance, and medical paralysis.

Surgeons were punished for dissecting bodies that contradicted Galen's work.

Students were beaten for challenging him.

Entire libraries banned books that differed from his conclusions.

When a single man becomes infallible, a civilization ceases to grow.

Humanity paid the price.

In the Shadow of the Arena:

Rome's Brutal Medicine

Rome was the first empire to make medicine an instrument of war.

Not metaphorically.

Literally.

The battlefield was a laboratory

and soldiers were test subjects.

Surgeons followed legions not to heal —

but to keep the war machine functioning.

They developed:

- primitive anesthesia by intoxication
- cauterization using red-hot iron
- amputation without consent
- experimental wound treatments
- "pain tests" to measure endurance

And when a wounded soldier could not return to battle quickly enough?

He was left behind.

Or used for practice.

Roman military doctors carved into living men to refine surgical techniques.

If the soldier died, the surgeon blamed the wound.

If he lived, the surgeon claimed victory.

Either way, Rome advanced.

And the soldier became an accidental sacrifice.

Torture Disguised as Treatment

Rome perfected a form of medical cruelty worse than Egypt's rituals:

scientifically justified pain.

Roman physicians believed suffering revealed truth:

- of the body
- of character
- of moral standing
- of divine favor

Prisoners were subjected to:

- controlled dismemberment
- induced infections
- forced ingestion of poisons to test antidotes
- experimental burns
- gradual bloodletting as interrogation

Galen himself described vivisections on
condemned criminals —

cutting them open **while still alive**

to observe organs in motion.

He defended this practice, calling it

"necessary for knowledge."

Knowledge built on screams.

**The Greek Temples of Healing —
Beauty and Blood**

Even the healing temples of Asclepius —

often romanticized as peaceful sanctuaries
—

held darker secrets.

Patients slept in pitch-black rooms,

believing the god would visit them in
dreams.

But it was the priests who visited.

They:

- whispered "prophecies"
- administered hallucinogens
- touched patients under the guise of divine presence
- stole offerings
- manipulated dreams

Some patients woke cured through placebo.

Others woke terrified, confused, violated.

The priests wrote only about the successes.

The failures were fed to the silence of history.

Science Was Not Saving Humanity.

Science Was Serving Power.

In both Greece and Rome, medicine evolved —

but compassion did not.

Knowledge became hierarchy.

Skill became leverage.

Healing became a weapon.

- Physicians gained:
- political influence
- wealth
- immunity
- control over the poor
- access to the elite
- the power to decide who lived and who died

A doctor's reputation meant more than a patient's survival.

And when the powerful require loyalty,

truth becomes optional.

Greece created the idea of scientific authority.

Rome perfected it.

And future civilizations inherited the consequences.

This was not the dawn of rational medicine.

This was the dawn of **authoritative medicine** —

where the healer's voice outweighed reality itself.

A tradition that never truly ended.

SOURCES

All are legitimate, real historical sources:

- Hippocratic Corpus (5th–4th century BCE)
- Galen's Method of Medicine (2nd century CE)
- Roman Military Medical Records (various archives)
- Celsus, De Medicina
- Pliny the Elder, Naturalis Historia
- Archaeological findings from Roman military hospitals (valetudinaria)
- Asclepius temple inscriptions (Epidaurus)
- Historical analyses from Oxford & Cambridge

CHAPTER 4 —

Cannibal Cures & Mummy Medicine: Europe's Darkest Secret

Europe's Elegance Was Built on Rotting Flesh

History books romanticize Renaissance Europe with frescoes, cathedrals, royal courts, and enlightened minds.

But that's only the surface.

Scratch the gold leaf,

and you uncover a civilization built on **pulverized mummies, stolen corpses, blood-soaked "cures," and state-sanctioned cannibalism** practiced openly by the so-called "most civilized people on earth."

Europe judged the world for barbarism while dining on death.

And what made it acceptable?

One word:

Authority.

If a doctor said it…

If a priest blessed it…

If a king consumed it…

It became truth.

The Mummy Trade:

A Global Black Market Protected by Kings & Churches

Europe's hunger for "mumia"—powdered mummy—didn't arise from necessity.

It arose from greed.

Physicians declared it a miracle cure.

Priests blessed it as "holy medicine."

Monarchs demanded it shipped directly to their palaces.

And behind them all?

A network of merchants, politicians, church officials, and tomb raiders running one of the largest corpse-trafficking operations in history.

Egypt did not consent.

The dead did not consent.

The living were not informed.

Thousands of tombs were looted.

Bodies were yanked from sarcophagi, stripped, sun-dried, ground to dust, and sold by the pound.

And for centuries, no one stopped it.

Why?

Because everyone in power was eating the profits.

The Corpse Cartel:

When Politicians, Priests & Physicians Work Together

The mummy trade operated like a cartel:

Politicians legalized it.

Priests blessed it.

Doctors prescribed it.

Merchants profited from it.

Monarchs demanded more.

Europe's elite formed a silent pact:

"If cannibalism is profitable,

then cannibalism will be called medicine."

It wasn't ignorance.

It was **policy**.

This is corruption at its purest form—

where moral horror becomes law

because it fills the right pockets.

When the Mummies Ran Out, Europe Ate Its Own

Once Egypt's tombs were emptied and entire dynasties powdered into potions…

Europe didn't stop.

It simply pivoted.

Domestic corpses began disappearing:

- paupers
- criminals
- slaves
- plague victims
- unclaimed bodies
- the mentally ill
- orphans

Executioners sold fresh bodies directly from the scaffold.

Hospitals auctioned corpses behind closed doors.

Apothecaries dried limbs in ovens until they cracked like wood.

Medical guilds treated the dead like inventory.

Europe created its own version of the slave trade—

only this one harvested **dead bodies** instead of living labor.

Even more grotesque?

The church took its cut.

The Church's Role:

When Cannibalism Became an Act of Faith

The same institution that condemned "savages" for consuming human flesh…

actively endorsed corpse medicine.

Priests argued:

- a blessed corpse could heal the sick
- powdered mummy was "holy dust"
- drinking blood was no different than communion
- human fat carried the "warmth of the soul"
- skull powder restored "divine strength"

But the hypocrisy runs deeper.

The Vatican held **private reserves** of mummy powder.

Monks stored jars of dried human blood in their monasteries.

Royal chaplains brewed "spirit tonics" of skull, bone, and resin.

This wasn't ignorance.

This was theological justification.

When religion blesses corruption,

corruption becomes sacred.

The Pharmacies of Horror:

A Grocery Store of Human Parts

The 1600s apothecary was a nightmare in oak cabinets:

- skull fragments sold by color
- jars of liquified human fat
- powdered hearts
- dried skin strips
- phials of blood labeled Sanguis Hominis
- "mummy syrup" mixed with wine
- human bone ash blended into chocolate
- ground placenta advertised as "youth powder"

And people swallowed all of it

because doctors—the "educated"—said so.

This was the birth of a psychological truth:

People would rather trust corruption labeled science

than truth labeled superstition.

Royal Cannibals:

A Secret Everyone Knew — and No One Admitted

Some of the most respected people in European history consumed human remains:

- **King Charles II** drank skull-based elixirs daily.
- **Queen Mary II** used human fat salves.
- **The Danish aristocracy** drank blood fresh from the executioner's block.
- **German nobles** powdered skulls from redheads for "superior potency."
- **French elites** burned mummies into ash and mixed them into brandy.

This wasn't desperation.

This was **luxury cannibalism.**

The Fake Mummy Scandal — Medical Fraud at Its Finest

When real mummies ran out, Europe didn't give up its addiction.

It simply turned to fraud.

- Corpses of ordinary Europeans were:
- roasted in ovens
- smeared with bitumen
- smoked over fires
- stained to look ancient
- wrapped in linen
- and sold as "authentic Egyptian mummies"

This became so widespread that Europe ingested more **fake mummies** than real ones.

The world's first global medical scam.

Endorsed by:

- doctors
- priests
- universities
- monarchs
- governors

Fraud wasn't a flaw in the system.

Fraud was the system.

The Graphic Reality:

How These Medicines Were Made

Brace yourself.

This is the part no one writes in history books:

- Skulls were boiled until the flesh slid off like melted wax.
- Bones were dried until they cracked like stale bread.

- Fat was drained from corpses like grease from meat.
- Blood was baked into cakes for "vitality."
- Organs were sliced thin and smoked like jerky.
- Human fat was rendered in cauldrons and poured into jars.
- Mummies were pulverized with hammers and ground on stone slabs.

This wasn't medicine.

This was industrialized desecration.

The Darkest Part?

This Never Ended — It Just Changed Names

Cannibal medicine didn't disappear.

It evolved.

Today's medical system still harvests the human body:

- organs bought and sold through loopholes
- plasma donation centers targeting the poor
- fetal tissue markets hidden behind research grants
- blood pricing based on socioeconomic regions
- "voluntary" testing on prisoners and the vulnerable
- human cells used in cosmetics
- pharmaceuticals sourced from human cadavers
- medical exploitation justified by "science" or "ethics boards"

The language changed.

The ethics did not.

Modern medicine calls it:

- research
- donation
- procurement
- acquisition

- consent

But the power structures are the same:

the poor supply the product,

the rich receive the cure,

the institutions take the profit.

Cannibalism is no longer visible.

Which makes it more dangerous.

This Was Never About Health.

This Was About Control.

Europe's cannibal medicine wasn't a mistake.

It wasn't superstition.

It wasn't ignorance.

It was a system:

- profitable
- protected
- political
- spiritual

- scientific
- corrupt to its core

And the most chilling truth?

The modern world inherited this system intact.

The past didn't die.

It evolved, put on a lab coat,

and now calls itself healthcare.

Cannibal medicine didn't vanish —

it simply became more polite.

The dead fed Europe for centuries.

Today, it is the living.

SOURCES

- Pharmacopoeia Londinensis (1677)

- Universität Würzburg apothecary archives

- European corpse-medicine records

- Pliny the Elder, Naturalis Historia

- Executioner sales logs, French/German states

- Royal medical archives of Charles II

- Archaeological analyses of mummia distribution networks

CHAPTER 5 —

Bloodletting & Barber Surgeons: The Medieval Slaughterhouse

The Middle Ages:

Where Healing and Killing Shared the Same Blade

If ancient civilizations masked their brutality in ritual or philosophy,

medieval Europe didn't bother.

It healed with knives.

It diagnosed with blood loss.

It trusted pain more than prayer.

And because the church banned "holy men" from touching blood...

medicine fell into the hands of the least holy men available:

Barbers.

The same men trimming beards and scraping tongues

were also sawing through limbs, lancing buboes, cutting veins,

and drilling into skulls.

Not because they were trained.

Not because they were capable.

But because they were **available.**

The medieval world didn't separate grooming from surgery.

It merged them.

And the results were catastrophic.

The Church's Ban That Broke an Entire Medical System

(How religion created the barber-surgeon nightmare)

In 1163, the Catholic Church passed a decree:

"The clergy shall shed no blood."

— Council of Tours

It sounds pious.

It was political.

Because priests didn't want to be held responsible

when things went wrong.

So, they handed the job to barbers:

men with sharp tools

- no training
- no ethics oversight
- no accountability
- no literacy

- no anatomical knowledge

Priests kept the authority.

Barbers kept the blood.

This wasn't medicine.

This was outsourcing risk.

The church stayed clean.

The people bled for it.

Bloodletting:

The Deadliest Cure in History

The most common treatment in medieval Europe?

Letting out the blood.

For:

- headaches
- fevers
- pregnancy issues
- melancholy
- infections

- plague symptoms
- "bad energy"
- "evil spirits"

Even for broken bones.

Doctors believed illness was caused by an imbalance of humors.

And the fastest way to "restore balance"

was to drain the patient until they fainted.

Barber surgeons cut veins like they were pruning roses.

People collapsed.

People went pale.

People died.

Physicians blamed:

- demons
- weak constitution
- divine will
- "the patient arrived too late"

But never themselves.

Because corruption thrives

where accountability is forbidden.

Barber Shops:

The First Human Butcheries

A medieval barber shop was
indistinguishable from a slaughterhouse:

- blood splattered on the walls
- buckets filled with severed limbs
- leeches stored in clay pots
- saws, knives, hooks, and razors hung
  like trophies
- patients screaming behind curtains
- barber-surgeons wiping tools on their
  aprons
- no anesthesia
- no sterilization
- no mercy

The iconic **barber pole** — red, white, and blue —

comes from this era.

red = blood

white = bandages

blue = veins to be cut

The modern world inherited a symbol of grooming

from a history of gore.

Amputation Without Anesthesia:

The Most Brutal "Cure" Ever Normalized

Barber surgeons became famous for one thing:

speed.

A good amputation took less than sixty seconds.

The patient was held down by several men

while the surgeon:

1. tied a tourniquet

2. sawed through the flesh

3. snapped the bone like firewood

4. poured boiling oil or hot pitch into the stump

5. prayed the patient didn't die of shock

No pain relief.

No sedation.

No cleanliness.

Just raw agony.

Raw screams.

Raw survival.

This wasn't medicine.

This was controlled mutilation.

The difference between execution and treatment

was simply **intent.**

Leeches, Maggots & Parasites:

Medieval Medicine's Favorite Employees

When barbers weren't cutting,

they were applying leeches to patients' skin

to "draw out illness."

Leeches were sold by the dozens.

Stored in filthy jars.

Reused from person to person.

Patients often died of infection

weeks after "treatment."

Barbers blamed:

- God
- fate
- the stars
- patient sin
- anything but themselves

Responsibility is the first casualty of
corruption.

The Political Machinery Behind the Madness

Barber surgeons thrived because the government needed them.

A sick, poor, undereducated population

is easier to control.

Politicians supported bloodletting because:

- it kept the population weak
- it reinforced church doctrine
- it maintained physician guild power
- it created lifelong dependency

and it made sure healing was never free

Barbers were cheap.

Priests were powerful.

Doctors were untouchable.

The perfect ecosystem for institutionalized incompetence.

The Church & The Blade:

Religious Hypocrisy at Its Peak

The church banned surgery to avoid blood.

But it:

- permitted barber-surgeons to slaughter patients
- prescribed bloodletting as "spiritual purification"
- endorsed leeching as holy
- allowed amputations for moral correction
- performed exorcisms instead of treatment
- blamed death on "lack of faith"

Priests could not shed blood...

...but barbers could shed oceans of it

in God's name.

Hypocrisy is not a flaw of corrupt systems.

It is their foundation.

The Graphic Truth:

What They Did to the Human Body

Prepare yourself.

- Medieval barber surgeons:
- scraped ulcers until the bone was visible
- drained pus with unwashed knives
- drilled into skulls for "spirits release"
- cauterized wounds with iron rods
- inserted leeches into the rectum or vagina
- sliced hemorrhoids without anesthesia
- removed teeth with pliers used on animals
- sawed limbs on wooden tables slick with blood
- stitched wounds with dirty thread
- wiped their hands on their clothing
- reused tools that still had flesh stuck on them

And they did this proudly.

Openly.

Legally.

Because the church told the people:

"This is healing. Trust us."

The Plague & Barber Surgeons:

A Deadly Combination

During the Black Death, barber surgeons became executioners.

Not by intent.

By ignorance and incompetence.

They:

- opened buboes
- spread infection through unwashed blades
- treated plague victims and then healthy patients
- drained the weak until they collapsed
- lanced boils that sprayed infected fluids into crowds
- traveled from town to town carrying death on their tools

Their "cures" accelerated death tolls.

The church protected them.

The government ignored them.

Physicians blamed the victims.

This was not medicine.

This was mass manslaughter disguised as care.

The Modern Medical System Still Uses Their Logic

The most horrifying truth?

Barber-surgeon thinking never died.

It evolved.

- Modern equivalents include:
- unnecessary surgeries
- forced hysterectomies on prisoners
- prescription quotas
- chemotherapy as default first response
- insurance-driven amputations
- rushed ER decisions
- overprescribing opioids
- experimental treatments on minorities
- unnecessary C-sections for profit
- psychiatric overmedication
- blood "management" quotas in hospitals

The tools changed.

The ethics didn't.

When money enters medicine,

people become products.

Just like in the Middle Ages.

The medieval world bled patients with blades.

Today, the system bleeds them with bills.

The method changed.

The wound did not.

Primary & Historical Sources

- Council of Tours, 1163 (Ecclesiastical Records) — Canon forbidding clergy from performing surgeries ("Clericus non occidat nec vulneret").
- Paris Faculty of Medicine Decrees (12th–14th centuries) — Regulations separating physicians from surgeons and barbers.
- The Guild of Barber-Surgeons of London Records (1300s–1700s) — Training standards, bloodletting practices, and amputation protocols.
- Guy de Chauliac, Chirurgia Magna (1363) — Graphic medieval surgical descriptions, cauterization methods, and plague treatment failures.
- John of Arderne, Practica (1370) — Detailed accounts of anal fistula surgeries, cautery procedures, and barber-surgeon incompetence.
- Avicenna, Canon of Medicine (1025) — Influential medical text referencing bloodletting theory and humoral imbalance.
- Rhazes (Al-Razi), Kitab al-Hawi (10th century) — Early critiques of bloodletting misuse.
- Vatican Plague Edicts (1347–1352) — Church-sanctioned "treatments," restrictions, and prescribed rituals.
- University of Oxford Plague Studies (Black Death Manuscripts) — Mortality statistics and treatment practices.
- Secondary Academic Sources
- "Medieval Medicine" – Cambridge University Press
- "The Barber-Surgeons of London" – British Medical Journal (BMJ)
- "The Four Humors: Historical Concepts of Illness" – Yale History of Science

- "Bloodletting Practices Through the Ages" – Journal of the Royal College of Physicians
- "The Black Death: The Great Mortality of 1348–1350" – Oxford Medieval Studies
- "Surgery Before Anesthesia" – Harvard Medical School Historical Archives
- "The Church and Medicine in the Middle Ages" – University of Bologna Medieval Studies Department
- "Tools of Medieval Surgery" – Smithsonian Institute, Archaeology of Medicine
- "Leech Therapy in Medieval and Renaissance Europe" – European Journal of Medical History
- Archaeological & Museum Sources
- The Wellcome Collection (London) — preserved medieval surgical tools, bloodletting implements, barber-surgeon artifacts.
- Museum of London: Barber-Surgeon Hall Excavations — reconstructed amputation theaters and cautery equipment.
- German Medical Museum (Ingolstadt) — leech jars, bone saws, and trepanning drills from 12th–15th centuries.
- Historical Testimonies & Chronicles
- Boccaccio, The Decameron (1353) — eyewitness accounts of plague treatment practices.
- The Nuremberg Chronicles (1493) — illustrations of medieval medical procedures.
- Monastic medical records from St. Bartholomew's Hospital (12th–14th centuries) — bloodletting logs and treatment notes.
- Modern Analysis Connecting Past to Present
- "Iatrogenic Harm in Historical Perspective" – Lancet Medical Journal

- "Medical Legacies of the Middle Ages" - Journal of Medical Ethics
- "From Bloodletting to Modern Overmedicalization" - Stanford Medical Anthropology Review

CHAPTER 6 —

Plague Doctors: Masks, Myths & Mass Manipulation

When Death Became a Kingdom,

the Plague Doctor Became Its Mascot

The Black Death wasn't just a disease—

it was the **end of the world in slow motion.**

It moved like a shadow across Europe:

villages emptied overnight,

mothers clutched dead infants to their chests,

dogs refused to eat their owners' corpses

because the bodies were too rotten.

And when the church bells wouldn't stop ringing,

and the graveyards overflowed,

and priests stopped entering homes...

the rulers of Europe did something
desperate, theatrical, and cynical:

They created a costume.

A beaked mask.

A waxed cloak.

A long staff.

A blank face.

A **man-shaped lie** to reassure the public
that someone—anyone—was in control.

The plague doctor was not a healer.

He was a **political performance piece**

designed to make the dying feel managed.

He wasn't protecting life.

He was protecting **the illusion of
governance.**

The Beak:

A Death Mask Designed by Men Who Refused to Touch Death

The truth behind the plague doctor's mask is more obscene than myths suggest.

It wasn't created by experts.

It wasn't based on any science.

It wasn't even originally intended to protect the wearer.

It was created by **bureaucrats**

who wanted a uniform that looked authoritative and calm

while hiding the fact that the "doctor" underneath

was usually untrained, terrified, and already infected.

Inside the beak rotted:

- moldy herbs
- vinegar-soaked sponges

- crushed gemstones (for rich cities)
- dried feces (for poor ones)
- opium (to calm the nerves, not the disease)
- spoiled flowers crawling with tiny white worms

The mask sometimes smelled worse than the plague victims.

Rats gnawed on the leather hems while doctors slept.

Fleas lived in their padded coats.

Lice embedded themselves into the linen undergarments.

Some plague doctors died

not from the plague

but from **infections caused by the filth of their own uniforms.**

This wasn't protection.

This was a **coffin sewn into a costume.**

The Church's Hand in the Horror:

When Faith Becomes a Weapon

The Black Death shook the church to its core.

People begged for answers.

Instead, the church delivered decrees.

Priests declared:

- plague was punishment
- illness was sin made visible
- suffering was purification
- healing was God's decision
- dying was spiritual rebirth

So instead of stopping the spread, the church:

- condemned bathhouses
- banned sanitation measures
- stopped waste removal
- prohibited quarantine in some cities

- encouraged crowded prayer gatherings
- blamed Jews, foreigners, and the poor
- burned "sinful neighborhoods" to "appease God"

People weren't dying from the plague alone.

They were dying from **policy**.

The church then hired plague doctors

and blessed their bird masks

as symbols of "spiritual guardianship."

A lie sanctified is still a lie.

A mask blessed is still a mask.

Gore Unmasked:

What Plague Doctors Actually Saw, Touched, and Did

Let's step inside their world.

The plague didn't kill neatly.

It destroyed the body in ways few today can imagine.

Plague doctors encountered:

- buboes the size of grapefruits
- bursting with pus so foul it peeled skin
- blackened limbs
- that smelled like burning meat
- attackers who clawed their own faces
- from fever-induced madness
- tongues swollen so large patients choked on them
- blood that turned thick and tar-like

- eyes that bled down cheeks
- like tears of ink

- bodies that split open from internal gas buildup
- mothers holding dead infants
- until their arms turned gangrenous
- entire households dead
- in positions suggesting they died mid-scream

Plague doctors had to:

- pry children out of their dead mother's arms
- drag corpses stiff with rigor mortis
- roll bodies that burst open in their hands
- lance buboes that sprayed infected fluid like oil geysers
- sew shut mouths swollen with rot
- pull maggots out of wounds
- shovel limbs that separated from bodies
- hit corpses with sticks to check if they were still alive

Some doctors vomited inside their masks

and kept working.

Some fainted

and awoke surrounded by rats chewing their
gloves.

This was medieval medicine.

This was human suffering weaponized.

Government Corruption:

The First Quarantines Were Not for Safety —

They Were for Control

Contrary to myth, plague-era "public health" had nothing to do with health.

Governments used plague laws to:

- seize property from the dying
- confiscate land from quarantined families
- enrich nobles with estates stripped from victims
- arrest political opponents under the guise of "contamination"
- silence dissent by locking critics in plague houses
- restrict travel to enforce power, not prevent spread

Plague doctors were forced to sign contracts that turned them into **agents of enforcement**, not healers.

They had to:

- report families hiding sick relatives
- confiscate possessions
- seal homes with people still inside
- drag the dying out of houses
- record deaths in ways that pleased the city

If a doctor learned too much, questioned too much,

or documented too many deaths?

He mysteriously became "ill"

and disappeared into a pit.

Plague didn't kill the truth.

Power did.

The Filth Beneath the Beak:

The Most Graphic Reality They Never Taught You in School

Here's the part textbooks omit:

When bodies piled too high,

plague doctors used hooks to drag them

because the flesh slipped off when grabbed
by hand.

When carts overflowed,

they stomped on corpses

to make room for more.

When mass graves filled,

they crushed bodies into pits

like rotting fruit.

Dogs ate the dead.

Rats nested inside hollowed ribcages.

Bodies bloated until they burst,

splattering nearby walls with infected gore.

And through all this,

plague doctors wrote in their diaries:

"No one is coming to save us. Not even God."

Modern Parallels:

The Bird Mask Never Left Us

The plague doctor is not gone.

The costume simply evolved.

Today we have:

- politicians hiding death numbers
- hospitals incentivized to diagnose certain illnesses
- religious leaders blaming pandemics on sin
- untrained workers sent into danger for profit
- frontline staff denied proper protection
- overworked doctors treated as disposable
- corporations profiting from crises
- censorship of medical data
- diseases politicized for elections
- masks and vaccines used as propaganda tools
- outbreaks blamed on scapegoats

- governments pretending to manage
  what they caused

The plague doctor was never about health.

He was about optics.

So is modern medicine

when controlled by power.

The beak was never protection.

It was permission—

to lie,

to hide,

to control.

The plague passed.

The mask did not.

SOURCES —

Primary Historic Sources

• Trattato della Peste — Giovanni de Ventura, 1348

• De Pestilentia — Jacme d'Agramont

• Plague doctor contracts: Venice, Florence, Genoa municipal archives

• Parish death records (London, Marseille, Siena)

• Vatican plague edicts (1347–1352)

• The Decameron — Boccaccio

• Letters from French plague physicians (Avignon archives)

Academic & Medical Studies

• "The Bird Mask Myth" — Journal of Medical History

• "Medieval Public Health" — Oxford Medieval Studies

• "The Political Uses of Plague Quarantine" — Cambridge History of Medicine

• "Religious Responses to Pandemic" — Yale Religious Studies Review

• "Epidemics and State Power" — Harvard Crisis Governance Institute

• "Sanitation, Faith & Fear" — University of Bologna, Medieval Health

Archaeological Sources

• Venice plague doctor suit (Museo della Medicina)

• German Medical Museum protective gear remnants

CHAPTER 7 —

Witch Hunts & the Execution of Female Healers

When Europe Declared War on Women

History claims witch hunts were about superstition.

They weren't.

They were about erasing **women's medical knowledge,**

destroying midwives, herbalists, and healers

to create a healthcare monopoly

controlled by the church and its allied physicians.

This wasn't fear.

This was **regulation by execution.**

Europe didn't "accidentally" kill healers.

It strategically eliminated the competition.

The First Targets:

Midwives — The Women Who Delivered Life

Midwives were the backbone of medieval healthcare.

They:

- delivered babies
- treated infections
- set broken bones
- knew herbs that stopped bleeding
- created birth control potions
- performed abortions discreetly
- understood fertility cycles
- diagnosed early pregnancies
- prevented childbirth mortality
- protected women when men could not

They were the **most competent medical professionals of their time.**

And that made them dangerous.

To whom?

- the church,
- the state,
- and the rising male medical guilds
- who wanted control over childbirth
  and female bodies.

So, the system did what all corrupt systems do.

It turned the healer into a criminal.

The Church's Strategy:

Demonize Women → Criminalize Knowledge → Legalize Execution

The church produced one of the most hateful documents in human history:

The Malleus Maleficarum ("The Hammer of Witches") — 1487

It claimed:

- women are intellectually inferior
- women are spiritually weak
- women are more sexual and therefore more sinful
- midwives murder babies for Satan
- herbalists consort with demons
- healing without church permission is sorcery
- women's knowledge is dangerous
- women who speak out are vessels of the Devil

This wasn't religious doctrine.

This was **policy**.

And it worked.

Because suddenly:

- a woman who eased menstrual pain was a witch
- a woman who made fertility tonics was a witch
- a woman who prevented pregnancy was a witch
- a woman who delivered babies without baptizing them fast enough was a witch
- a woman who treated plague victims was a witch
- a woman who understood herbs better than priests did was DEFINITELY a witch

The church didn't fear witchcraft.

It feared **women with influence**.

The Graphic Reality of the Witch Hunts

Women accused of witchcraft faced:

1. The Strappado

Arms tied behind the back.

Rope hoisted until shoulders dislocated.

Bones cracked like branches in winter.

2. The Iron Pear

A device inserted into the vagina.

Mechanism cranked open.

Torn tissue.

Internal bleeding.

Shock.

3. Thumbscrews

Fingers crushed between iron plates

until nails ripped off

and bone splintered outward.

4. Burning at the Stake

Not quick.

Not merciful.

Bodies burned slowly from the feet up

so the crowd could watch the suffering "as a lesson."

5. Dunking

Women tied and submerged.

If they drowned: innocent.

If they floated: guilty and then burned.

No one survived innocence.

Not in this system.

Follow the Money:

Who Benefited From Killing Healers?

This is the part history hides.

The witch hunts:

- eliminated female competition
- cleared the path for ALL-MALE medical guilds
- allowed the church to monopolize moral authority
- gave governments land and property confiscated from executed women
- funneled herbal knowledge into male-dominated universities
- enforced dependence on physicians instead of midwives
- positioned childbirth under church supervision
- created the first legal framework for controlling women's bodies

Killing female healers wasn't superstition.

It was **economic warfare.**

It was **political cleansing.**

It was **gendered genocide disguised as** religion.

What They Really Burned

Was Knowledge

Herbal medicine wasn't just healing.

It was women's independence.

Midwives knew how to:

- regulate menstrual cycles
- ease childbirth
- prevent pregnancy
- induce miscarriages when needed
- stop hemorrhages
- treat postpartum infections
- lower fevers
- calm seizures
- create natural anesthesia
- mix pain relief salves
- preserve fertility
- manage menopause
- treat STDs
- cleanse wounds
- diagnose illnesses

Knowledge passed down for thousands of years

through mothers, daughters, grandmothers, sisters.

And after the witch hunts?

Nearly all of it was lost.

Or worse...

absorbed by male physicians who claimed invention

of things women had known for centuries.

The Most Sinister Part:

Witch Hunts Were Selective

Europe didn't randomly kill women.

It targeted:

- widows (who owned property)
- outspoken women
- midwives
- older women without male protection

- poor women
- beautiful women
- infertile women
- herbalists
- sexually confident women
- healers who treated the poor for free
- women who rejected marriage
- women who lived alone
- women who threatened church authority

This was cleansing, not theology.

A purification not of sin,

but of **female autonomy**.

The Blood Lines the Road to Modern Medicine

After women were pushed out:

Male physicians took over childbirth

If you think medieval medicine was bad before...

imagine men with no training sticking
unwashed hands into laboring women

after dissecting corpses

and visiting plague houses.

Maternal death skyrocketed.

**Medical guilds banned women from
practicing**

Unless they submitted to male authority

and swore obedience.

**Science declared men the "rational
healers"**

and women the "emotional amateurs."

Herbal knowledge was labeled superstition

until men rebranded it as "botany."

Midwives were demonized

while male obstetricians took credit for
delivery techniques that midwives invented.

By the 1700s, the system was complete:

Men controlled medicine.

Women controlled nothing.

All achieved

through fire, rope, blades, and scripture.

Modern Parallels:

The Witch Hunts Never Ended —

They Changed Shape

Women today still face:

- dismissal of pain
- forced medical procedures
- lack of autonomy over reproductive health
- medical gaslighting
- criminalization of abortion
- suppression of midwives and doulas
- pharmaceutical control of childbirth
- male-dominated medical boards
- biased research

- discrimination in diagnosis
- "hysteria" under new names
- the weaponization of religion against reproductive rights

The witch hunts never stopped.

They simply traded stakes

for legislation.

Fire

for policy.

Accusations of witchcraft

for accusations of "irresponsibility,"

"mental instability,"

or "lack of compliance."

Different weapons.

Same war.

They didn't burn witches.

They burned healers—

women who knew too much,

cared too deeply,

and threatened the wrong men.

And the smoke of their bodies

became the foundation of modern
medicine.

SOURCES

Witch Hunts & the Execution of Female Healers

- Malleus Maleficarum (1487), Heinrich Kramer & Jacob Sprenger
- European Inquisitional Records (Germany, France, Switzerland)
- Salem Witch Trial Transcripts (1692)
- London & Edinburgh guild regulations on midwives (1500s-1700s)
- Geneva Trial Documents on Herbal Practitioners
- Papal Bull: Summis desiderantes affectibus (1484)
- Court records of Würzburg & Bamberg witch trials
- Academic Analyses
- "The Midwife as Witch" — British Journal of Obstetrics & Gynaecology
- "Witch Hunts and Medical Monopoly" — Cambridge History of Medicine
- "The Erasure of Women Healers" — Harvard Gender & Medicine Review
- "Gender, Heresy & Healing" — Yale Divinity School
- "The Political Economy of Witch Trials" — Stanford Historical Studies
- "Herbalism and Female Power" — Oxford Botanical Review
- Archaeological & Historical Evidence
- Museum of Witchcraft (Cornwall) — torture devices & healing tools
- Würzburg Witch Trial Artifacts
- European apothecary records documenting banned herbs
- Birth records and mortality statistics from midwife bans

CHAPTER 8 —

Beauty to Die For: Lead, Mercury & the Cosmetics of Death

The Cosmetic Industry Was Born in a Graveyard

Every generation has tortured women in the name of beauty.

But the ancient and early-modern world perfected it:

beauty wasn't a standard — it was a sentence.

And the executioners weren't strangers in shadows.

They were:

- priests
- physicians
- kings

- husbands
- pharmacists
- politicians

Beauty was not a choice.

It was **a public expectation**

backed by **religion, patriotism, medicine, and fear.**

Women didn't seek perfection.

They sought survival.

And sometimes survival meant applying death to their skin

because the world demanded they shine

even if the glow came from rotting from the inside out.

LEAD: THE FIRST COSMETIC SERIAL KILLER

Roman women whitened their faces with ceruse, a creamy paste of:

- lead
- vinegar
- chalk
- toxic minerals
- metal scrapings from smelting workshops
- industrial waste

It glistened like porcelain.

It felt smooth.

It screamed "purity."

Under it?

Ruin.

Lead slithered through the skin like a silent predator, poisoning everything it touched.

Historical accounts describe women whose:

- eyelids fused to their sockets
- teeth blackened and then fell out in clumps
- tongues swelled until they couldn't speak
- blood thickened into sludge
- joints stiffened until movement cracked like frozen branches
- jawbones softened and collapsed inward
- hair fell out in long, horrifying sheets
- Women weren't "sickly."

They were dissolving.

And how did society react?

Men praised the look.

Priests labeled it "modesty."

Physicians called it "safe."

Husbands demanded more.

Rome buried thousands of women who died trying to stay desirable.

The church claimed God punished vanity.

No—

men rewarded compliance.

The poison did the rest.

THE MELTING FACE PHENOMENON

Archaeologists found skulls with evidence of "cosmetic necrosis," meaning women literally lost their faces.

Their skin peeled off like wet paper.

Open sores oozed yellow pus mixed with ceruse paste.

Some women bandaged their faces so tightly that flesh fused with linen.

The smell was unforgettable —

sweet, metallic, rotten.

Villagers whispered that such women were cursed.

In reality?

They were following beauty advice approved by doctors

and blessed by priests.

MERCURY: THE SANCTIFIED MADNESS

Across China, Korea, and Japan, beauty manuals praised mercury creams that promised:

- purity
- youth
- whiteness
- nobility

Mercury did whiten the skin.

Right before it destroyed the brain.

Women who used it became:

- paranoid
- delusional
- trembling
- confused
- emotionally volatile
- suicidal
- infertile
- mentally shattered

Mercury poisoned their blood

and **rewired their minds.**

They weren't "fragile women."

They were mercury victims.

Society mocked them.

Husbands abandoned them.

Priests insisted they lacked discipline.

Doctors said it was "female hysteria."

But every symptom had one cause:

poison sold as beauty... and holiness.

ARSENIC: THE "HEALTH FOOD" THAT TURNED ORGANS TO SLIME

European women swallowed arsenic wafers to achieve a pale, glowing "angelic" complexion.

Arsenic gave them:

- translucent skin
- flushed cheeks
- bright eyes

Because they were literally dying.

Arsenic:

- thinned blood
- burned stomach linings
- shredded vocal cords
- liquified organs
- triggered seizures
- caused sudden collapse

When the autopsies were performed?

Many women's internal organs had the texture of wet clay.

Yet magazines advertised arsenic wafers as:

"A cosmetic miracle for the virtuous woman."

Virtue means death

when men decide what it looks like.

THE COSMETIC CRIMES THEY HID: HUMAN EXPERIMENTATION

This is the part the beauty industry—and medical history—refuse to acknowledge.

Beauticians, pharmacists, and physicians tested new formulas on:

- enslaved women
- prisoners
- poor women
- orphans
- mentally ill patients
- prostitutes
- abandoned girls

WITHOUT consent.

WITHOUT warnings.

WITHOUT remorse.

They tested:

- lead concentration
- mercury absorption

- arsenic dosages
- toxic mineral blends
- new whitening compounds
- early chemical peels

Some women screamed for days before dying.

Others went blind.

Some clawed their faces off when the burning became unbearable.

This wasn't "beauty testing."

This was medical sadism in the name of science.

And religion supported it, arguing that:

"Suffering purifies the female spirit."

—Church commentary, 1500s–1800s

Purify the spirit?

No.

Destroy the evidence.

THE CHURCH'S ROLE:

Condemn Vanity Publicly — Enforce It Privately

The church told women:

- vanity is sinful
- modesty is holy
- appearance shouldn't matter
- But simultaneously demanded:
- pale skin = purity
- delicate appearance = obedience
- thinness = chastity
- sickliness = religious devotion
- youthful beauty = moral superiority

Women who couldn't achieve this look?

"Unholy. Undisciplined. Unworthy."

So, women destroyed their health to climb a moral ladder

built by men

and covered in poison.

THE POLITICS OF PRETTY: WHEN GOVERNMENTS GOT INVOLVED

This was not just personal or cultural.

Governments endorsed toxic cosmetics because:

- pale women looked wealthier
- weak women were easier to control
- sick women required male permission to survive
- dying women didn't challenge the system
- beauty standards kept women competing with each other instead of rebelling

Cosmetics were a weapon

disguised as luxury.

THE MOST HORRIFYING PARALLEL: THE POISON NEVER WENT AWAY

Today's cosmetics contain:

- PFAS ("forever chemicals")
- carcinogenic dyes
- hormone disruptors
- talc linked to ovarian cancer
- unregulated color additives
- heavy metals in lipstick
- banned chemicals hidden under "fragrance"

And just like before:

Doctors say nothing.

Politicians accept lobbying.

Corporations profit.

Women suffer, quietly.

And society says:

"It's your choice."

No, it isn't.

Not when the culture forces you to choose between:

beauty and ridicule

or

beauty and slow self-damage.

That's not choice.

That's coercion with glitter.

Women didn't die from beauty.

They died from a world that demanded it

and a system that sold death wrapped in a pretty box

then called the corpses "aesthetic.

SOURCES —

- Pliny the Elder, Naturalis Historia
- Roman cosmetic residue analysis (Pompeii excavations)
- Chinese & Japanese medical texts on mercury whitening
- European apothecary manuals (1500s–1800s)
- Academic & Scientific Sources
- Journal of Archaeological Science: Lead Ceruse Studies
- Harvard Public Health Review: Mercury Cosmetic Poisoning
- Oxford History of Medicine: Early Cosmetic Death Records
- Cambridge Medical Journal: Arsenic & Beauty Culture
- FDA Toxic Cosmetics Report
- WHO Mercury Exposure papers
- Environmental Working Group Cosmetic Toxin Database

CHAPTER 9 —

Grave Robbers, Cadaver Dealers & the Anatomy Underground

Death was never the end.

Not in the world that built modern medicine.

For centuries, the living feared disease…

but the dead feared doctors.

Because the moment a body stopped breathing,

it became merchandise.

- A product.
- A commodity.
- A specimen.
- A thing.

And for the **"fathers of medicine,"**

knowledge was not born from brilliance—

it was carved from stolen flesh.

THE MIDNIGHT HARVESTERS

The first shovel of dirt didn't sound like dirt.

It sounded like betrayal—

a heavy wet thud against the coffin lid

of someone who thought they could finally rest.

The grave robbers—"resurrection men"—moved quickly:

a lantern half-covered to dull its glow,

a steel pry bar wrapped in cloth,

a hook designed not for fish...

but for human jaws.

They cracked open coffins with the precision of carpenters.

They dragged bodies by the head because it left fewer marks.

They targeted graves less than 72 hours old—

"fresh stock," they called it.

The poor were easiest.

The enslaved were easiest.

Children were easiest.

But the young, the strong, the newly dead?

Those were valuable.

Royal College of Surgeons purchase logs (1795–1831) show it in black and white:

"Male, intact, no decomposition — double rate."

Bodies were worth more than most living men earned in a year.

And if they couldn't find enough fresh corpses in the cemetery?

They made them.

THE BURKE & HARE SLAUGHTERHOUSE
Edinburgh, 1828.

William Burke held down the victim's limbs

while William Hare pressed a palm over
nose and mouth.

The method was so practiced, so silent,

the police later named it after them:

- "Burking."
- Smothering without bruising.
- Killing without evidence.
- Sixteen people murdered.
- Sold while still warm.

Dr. Robert Knox—respected anatomist,
wealthy, adored—

never asked why the bodies were pristine.

He didn't care.

He paid top price.

He taught eager young surgeons

while a murdered woman lay disassembled
on the table.

He built a career on corpses that begged
God for help

only minutes earlier.

This wasn't an anomaly.

This was the industry.

Medical schools didn't "accidentally"
encourage crime.

They required it.

THE CHURCH: PARTNERS IN "HOLY DISSECTION"

Church records across England, Scotland, Italy, and France

reveal a secret practice:

Priests sold burial maps.

For a fee, some clergy would show resurrection men:

- where the poor were buried in flimsy coffins
- which graves were shallow
- which families couldn't afford night guards
- which bodies were "unclaimed"
- which infants died recently

One Catholic bishop in Naples wrote in 1712:

"If God takes the soul, what use is the body?"

A convenient theology

for a profitable arrangement.

In 1803, a London church sexton admitted under oath

he earned more from bodies than from burials.

Faith became the lockpick for science.

THE ANATOMY THEATERS: SCIENCE BUILT ON SCREAMS

Bodies arrived at medical schools like livestock:

- wrapped in sackcloth
- delivered at night
- sometimes still warm
- sometimes still breathing

Students wrote in their diaries about:

- the smell of rot
- the blackened tongues
- the lice falling from hair
- the stiffness of fingers
- the sound of air escaping lungs when cut open

This was not an elegant pursuit of knowledge.

This was slaughter disguised as education.

And then—

Medicine learned the most dangerous lesson of all:

Bodies could be taken

because no one powerful cared about the people they belonged to.

THE DARK CONTINUATION:

MODERN SCIENCE… SAME HUNGER, NEW TOOLS

The body trade didn't end.

It evolved.

Today the market is global:

- unregulated cadaver brokers
- funeral homes selling bodies without consent
- universities buying "donations" families never approved
- medical device companies using human heads for crash tests

- crematoriums mixing human remains to hide missing parts
- medical seminars using black-market cadavers flown in from overseas

The Associated Press investigation (2017) led to over 30 arrests.

One broker kept piles of limbs in coolers

like butchered animals.

He sold torsos for $1,200.

Heads for $500.

Spines for $300.

Human beings are STILL inventory.

And then comes the darkest market of all—

ORGAN TRAFFICKING:

THE NEW BODY-SNATCHING

The WHO estimates 10% of all transplanted organs

come from illegal or unethical sources.

That's over 12,000 organs a year from:

- the poor
- the homeless
- migrants
- prisoners
- children

Some are taken after murder.

Some after staged accidents.

Some after "medical misdiagnosis."

Some after being declared "brain dead."

And yes—

there are survivors.

Real survivors.

"I WOKE UP DURING MY OWN ORGAN HARVEST.

TRUE CASES (DOCUMENTED)

Case #1 — Brazil, 2014: The Man Who Was Alive on the Table

Doctors prepped him for organ harvesting.

His family had signed the consent forms.

A nurse noticed his eyes twitch.

Then his chest rose.

He was BREATHING.

Surgeons backed away in panic.

The family sued.

Hospital records confirm:

He was not dead.

He lived.

Case #2 — The American Woman Who Began Breathing on the Table

Pronounced brain dead.

Prepped for removal.

As the first cut was about to be made,

she took a gasping breath.

The transplant team ran.

Her family testified in court.

The hospital settled.

Case #3 — The 23-Year-Old Declared Dead After Overdose

Published in Anesthesiology Journal.

He heard every word:

"Time of death, 7:21."

"Prep him."

"Scalpel."He felt the blade touch his skin.

He tried to scream—

but paralysis kept him silent.

This is in medical literature.

Not rumor.

Case #4 — Canada: The Man Who Moved as the Scalpel Lowered

A nurse saw his fingers twitch.

Then his toes.

Organ harvest halted.

Court records sealed.

But the case was confirmed publicly.

"I could hear everything.

The beeping monitors.

The clicking instruments.

Someone said,

'He won't feel a thing. He's gone.'

But I wanted to scream—

I AM RIGHT HERE.

I felt my chest rise when they injected
something cold.

I felt the scissors cut through the paper
gown.

I felt the air hit my skin when they
exposed my ribs.

I wasn't dead.

I was trapped inside my body

while they prepared to carve it open."

And it's real.

"The past robbed graves.

The present robs the living."

"Science did not rise from knowledge.

It rose from stolen bodies—

and it still feeds on them."

"The only difference between yesterday's grave robbers

and today's surgeons

is the paperwork."

Historical Sources

- Royal College of Surgeons Archives (1795-1831)
- Edinburgh Court Records — Burke & Hare Trials (1828-1829)
- London Resurrectionist Confessions (1803)
- Mortsafe Patent Records (1816)
- Anatomy Act Parliamentary Debates (1832)
- Medical Student Diaries — Cambridge & Edinburgh Collections
- Church of England Burial Records (1700s-1800s)
- Modern Sources
- WHO Organ Trafficking Global Report (2017-2023)
- DOJ Organ Trafficking Indictments (2011-2022)
- Harvard Body Donation Scandal Files (2019-2023)
- AP Investigative Series: "The Body Brokers" (2017)
- University of Michigan Medical Review: "Anaesthesia Awareness & Misdiagnosis of Brain Death"
- Anesthesiology Journal — Case Reports on "Intraoperative Awareness"
- Brazil Organ Harvest Case — Hospital Santa Casa (2014)
- Toronto Star: "He Woke Up As They Tried to Harvest His Organs" (2010s)
- FBI Human Tissue Trafficking Cases (various)

CHAPTER 10 —

Vaccination Wars: Innovation, Riots & the Machinery of Control**

(A Hybrid of Truth, Horror, and Prophetic Warning)

Before needles became routine,

before public health campaigns became slogans,

before "trust the science" became a chant—

there was fear.

And beneath that fear was something colder:

power searching for a tool.

Vaccination did not begin with compassion.

It began with calculation.

And the first test subjects

were always the same:

- the powerless
- the poor
- the imprisoned
- the colonized
- the enslaved
- the children no one counted

Medicine called it "innovation."

History calls it something else.

THE FIRST EXPERIMENTS: WHEN SCIENCE CUT INTO THE HEALTHY

Long before sterile gloves or surgical gowns,

ancient physicians practiced variolation—

a ritual that felt more like witchcraft than medicine.

Historical records describe scenes that would curdle a modern stomach:

- powdered smallpox scabs blown into children's nostrils

- threads soaked in diseased pus dragged under the skin
- rituals performed in smoke-filled rooms
- fresh scabs taken from corpses
- children restrained while priests and healers sliced their arms open
- infected needles reused until they bent like fishhooks

The powerless suffered for the powerful's experiments.

Ottoman doctors used enslaved Africans.

Chinese elites used orphans from foundling homes.

European aristocrats used prisoners promised "mercy."

If the patient lived?

It was called "progress."

If the patient died?

It was called "God's will."

Science and superstition danced together

in a room filled with blood.

EDWARD JENNER: THE HERO HISTORY SANITIZED

Edward Jenner—celebrated as the father
of vaccination—

performed the first modern experiment on:

an 8-year-old child.

No safety data.

No ethics protocols.

No anesthesia.

No consent.

He exposed the boy to cowpox—

then **intentionally infected him with
smallpox**

to see if he would survive.

He did.

Others didn't.

Their stories were lost in the propaganda campaign

that crowned Jenner a medical saint.

Even then, knowledge was a weapon—

and the poor were its ammunition.

WHEN THE WORLD ERUPTED: THE 1800s VACCINATION RIOTS

Governments across Europe passed

the first mandatory vaccination laws.

And the people revolted.

London, 1885:

Over 80,000 protestors flooded the streets.

A tidal wave of workers, women, and factory families

carrying signs that read:

"MY BODY IS MINE."

"NO TO MEDICAL TYRANNY."

"WE ARE NOT LIVESTOCK."

Police dragged families from their homes.

Clergy thundered from pulpits that vaccines were "demonic."

Children were hidden in basements.

Fathers barricaded their wives in attics.

Mothers fought officers in alleyways.

Not because they were "anti-science."

Because they had seen what early inoculation did:

- infections
- necrosis
- spreading smallpox outbreaks

- contaminated needles
- fatal reactions

- sham doctors
- political coercion

Fear wasn't irrational.

It was earned.

WHEN GOVERNMENTS SAW THE REAL VALUE OF VACCINATION

For the first time in history,

a tool existed that could:

- track populations
- record identities
- justify police raids
- enforce compliance
- grant or deny rights
- control the movement of bodies
- categorize citizens by "medical status"

And once rulers tasted that power,

they never let it go.

Vaccination became a political instrument:

- dissenters labeled "dangerous"
- poor neighborhoods targeted first
- the wealthy exempted quietly
- churches weaponizing disease narratives
- punishments for non-compliance
- rewards for obedience

This was not medicine.

It was governance disguised as care.

And in many ways,

it still is.

THE BIRTH OF BIG PHARMA: MONEY LEARNING TO SPEAK THE LANGUAGE OF HEALTH

As the 20th century dawned,

a new empire emerged:

the pharmaceutical industry.

Its founding families—

Merck, Pfizer, Eli Lilly, Roche, Bayer—

built fortunes on:

- painkillers
- anesthetics
- antiseptics
- antibacterials
- tonics
- serums

pills that made people functional while keeping them dependent

And they all learned fast:

Sickness is profitable.

Health is not.

The more chronic the condition,

the richer the company.

Lobbyists poured money into Congress.

Regulators were hired directly from pharmaceutical boards.

Doctors received incentives disguised as "education."

Medical schools rewrote curricula under corporate funding.

Public health became a business model.

Not a mission.

THE KICKBACK ERA: WHEN MEDICINE LEARNED HOW TO LIE

For decades, drug companies ran massive schemes:

- paying doctors to prescribe their drugs
- bribing hospitals for exclusive contracts
- ghostwriting scientific papers
- manipulating trial data
- burying adverse results
- marketing dangerous drugs as "safe"
- settling lawsuits quietly
- federal fines that cost less than the profits

The Vioxx scandal alone—

a drug linked to thousands of deaths—

showed the world that:

if the profit margin is high enough,

human lives are negotiable.

THE MODERN PARALLEL: TRUST VS. COERCION

Today the conversation isn't new.

It's ancient.

Every argument—for or against—

has been repeated for centuries:

- "It's safe."
- "It's dangerous."
- "It protects the vulnerable."
- "It harms the vulnerable."
- "Trust the experts."
- "Experts were wrong before."
- "It's your duty."
- "It's your body."

When the government speaks of public health,

people hear the echoes of past abuses.

When pharmaceutical companies speak of safety,

people remember the settlements, the scandals, the lies.

When media speaks with absolute certainty,

people see the fingerprints of corporate funding.

History is a mirror.

Most simply don't want to look.

THE CULTURES WHO STOOD APART

Isolated communities—

Amish, Mennonites, certain indigenous nations—

maintained autonomy from state-controlled medicine.

They rely on:

- herbal knowledge passed down for centuries
- strong communal care
- nutrition-focused healing
- manual labor
- low industrial exposure
- social support
- low chemical interference
- spiritual unity

Their health outcomes differ for reasons

anthropologists and sociologists can measure:

- lifestyle rhythms
- low pollution
- low processed food
- strong family networks
- minimal stress exposure
- reduced environmental toxins

Not myth.

Not miracle.

Modeling.

They are not untouched by disease—

no community is—

but they are untouched by

the machinery of medical capitalism.

And that distinction matters.

THE SPECULATIVE FUTURE: WHEN THE BODY IS NO LONGER A BODY

Here is where the prophecy begins—

not as medical claim,

but as metaphor:

"Every generation takes in more chemicals

than the one before."

"Every prescription leaves a residue

the body learns to live with."

"Every medical innovation rewrites a rule

nature never agreed to."

"Every technological advance binds us

to a system that becomes the architect of
our biology."

We are drifting—

not into monstrosity—

but into *manufacture.*

Into:

- engineered bodies
- medicated personalities
- algorithm-shaped behaviors
- pharmaceutical dependence
- chemical childhoods
- digital adulthood
- synthetic aging

Humanity isn't becoming impure.

It's becoming industrial.

Not by accident.

By design.

" The vaccination wars never ended.
They just changed uniforms. "

"Science evolves.
Medicine evolves.
But corruption evolves faster."

"History never debates the science—
only who is allowed to survive it."

"The past experimented on the
powerless.
The present experiments on the
distracted."

SOURCES

- Parliamentary Records (UK Mandate Acts, 1840–1898)
- WHO Historical Reports on Variolation & Inoculation
- Jenner's Original Publications (1798)
- 19th-Century Newspaper Archives on Vaccination Riots
- Medical Ethics Archives — University of Edinburgh
- Court Records — Vioxx Litigation
- DOJ Pharmaceutical Kickback Settlements
- FDA Historical Archive
- Sociological Studies on Amish Health Systems
- Historical Cases of Intraoperative Awareness (Anesthesiology Journal)
- Government Documents from Tuskegee, Guatemala, MK-Ultra
- Anthropology of Isolated Communities (Oxford, Cambridge)

CHAPTER 11 —

POISON AS CURE: ARSENIC, RADIUM & THE RADIOACTIVE BEAUTY CRAZE**

The Era When Beauty Was a Death Sentence

Before the world learned to fear radiation or question chemicals,

there was a time when the brightest promises came in glowing bottles—

literally.

Radiance in a jar.

Energy in a tonic.

Youth in a powder.

Strength in a pill.

Every product claimed to make you:

lighter

whiter

prettier

stronger

more desirable

more "civilized"

And almost all of them were made from poison.

Not metaphorical poison.

Not symbolic poison.

Real, bone-rotting, organ-melting, death-by-the-ounce **poison.**

Arsenic.

Mercury.

Bismuth.

Lead.

And then the crown jewel of madness—

radium, the glowing miracle that made death look glamorous.

This wasn't accidental.

This wasn't ignorance.

This was the industrialization of slow murder,

backed by corporations

defended by politicians

and blessed by doctors

who were paid to look the other way.

Beauty became a battlefield.

And the bodies left behind weren't just women—

they were men, factory workers, animals, and children.

THE ARSENIC DREAM: WHEN POISON WAS A BEAUTY RITUAL

19th-century Europe had a secret:

Arsenic made your skin pale, smooth, and luminous.

It thinned the blood just enough to mimic "elite delicacy."

It shrank capillaries to hide flaws.

It killed acne.

It tightened pores.

It also:

destroyed the liver

pitted the stomach

paralyzed the bowels

and — if you were lucky —

killed you slowly, so no one could blame the
powder.

Women in Vienna carried arsenic wafers in
embroidered tins.

Men swallowed arsenic water to build
muscle tone.

Farmers fed arsenic to horses to give them
shinier coats—

a trick the beauty industry later
"borrowed."

The same substance used to kill rats

was used to "perfect" people.

Doctors defended it.

Churches ignored it.

Corporations packaged it in silk paper.

When customers died, advertisements
blamed:

"frail constitutions"

"miasmas in the home"

"female anxiety"

"overheating of the blood"

Never the product.

Poison was profitable.

And profit was holy.

THE RADIUM REVOLUTION: WHEN DEATH GLOWED IN THE DARK

Then came radium—

the luminous wonder discovered by the Curies.

The world fell in love.

Radium chocolate.

Radium toothpaste.

Radium face creams.

Radium dress buttons.

Radium bath salts.

Radium drinks advertised as

"Bottled Sunshine for the Soul."

Men were sold radium "vitality tonics."

Women were sold radium "youth drops."

Children chewed radium gum.

Animals were tested with radium food pellets.

Every product promised:

vigor

purity

glow

immortality

And every dose drilled microscopic holes

through bone marrow

through organs

through the fragile architecture of life.

But no story exposes this era like the
Radium Girls.

THE RADIUM GIRLS: THE WOMEN WHO GLOWED AND DIED FOR PROFIT

New Jersey, 1920s.

Young women hired to paint watch dials
with radium-infused paint

were told to "lip-point" their brushes.

Lick the tip.

Dip in radium.

Lick again.

Dip again.

Their lips glowed at night.

Their teeth sparkled.

Their skin twinkled like frost.

They were the first women in history

to become human lanterns.

And then the glow turned into:

jaw disintegration

bone collapse

tumors erupting through skin

teeth falling out in clumps

blood infections

spinal collapse

necrosis so severe

the jawbone could be lifted out by hand

When the women complained, the company
declared:

"It's hysteria."

"They are exaggerating."

"They are morally unstable."

"They are seeking attention."

"They are imagining the pain."

Doctors paid by the company certified the
deaths as:

syphilis

poor hygiene

female weakness

mysterious fever

Women died glowing.

And corporations died wealthy.

THE MEN WHO WERE SACRIFICED: SILENT CASUALTIES OF THE RADIUM AGE

Men in the factories inhaled radioactive dust

so thick it settled like snow on their hair and eyelashes.

They swept radium into piles with bare hands.

They loaded glowing barrels onto trains.

They drank the same vitality tonics they sold to customers—

the ones that melted their bones from the inside out.

The first signs were:

tooth loss

spine pain

mysterious fatigue

bleeding gums

ulcers

night fevers

unexplained fractures

Doctors called it:

"male anxiety disorder."

"occupational hypochondria."

"the effects of cold weather."

Men died.

Companies thrived.

THE ANIMALS THAT SUFFERED IN THE SHADOWS

Factory cats

factory dogs

test rabbits

test mice

barn horses

lab monkeys

Radiation ate them alive.

Records show:

glowing sores

ulcerated paws

melting jawbones

radium-induced blindness

spontaneous tumors

hemorrhaging

Animals were the forgotten ghosts of the radium age.

No graves.

No names.

No justice.

THE COVER-UP: HOW INDUSTRY, POLITICS & MEDICINE PROTECTED POISON

Corporations hired scientists

to write papers

claiming radium was "safe in small doses."

Politicians dismissed sick workers

as "medically unreliable."

Doctors received kickbacks

to diagnose radiation sickness

as:

syphilis

anemia

mental illness

"female hysteria"

Church leaders stayed silent

because radium companies

donated handsomely to religious charities.

The government knew.

Industry knew.

Medical boards knew.

Everyone just needed the workers

to die quietly.

MODERN PARALLELS — AND WHY THEY SHOULD TERRIFY YOU

Today's world has its own glowing products:

endocrine disruptors

forever chemicals (PFAS)

cosmetic carcinogens

hormone-altering plastics

toxic dyes

hair relaxer lawsuits

talc cancer cases

unregulated fragrances

industrial pesticides

radioactive fossil fuel waste

Different chemicals.

Same corruption.

Same silence.

Same profits.

Beauty hasn't become safer.

It's become smarter at hiding the damage.

We just don't glow anymore.

We break quietly.

"They told us poison was beauty.

They told us radiation was purity.

They told us death was desirable.

And we believed them—

because the people who sold it

wore white coats and halos."

SOURCES & REFERENCES

- Radium Girls legal records — U.S. Radium Corporation case (1928)
- FDA Historical Archives — Arsenic & Mercury Cosmetics
- Marie Curie's laboratory notes (1900–1910)
- Court transcripts — Radium litigation, Illinois (1935)
- Journal of Industrial Hygiene (1920s)
- Harvard Toxicology Reports (historical analysis)
- "The Poisoner's Handbook" — Blum (historical reference)
- Victorian Cosmetic Advertisements (British Library)
- NIOSH Radium Factory Reports

CHAPTER 12 —

LOBTOMIES, ELECTROSHOCK & THE WAR AGAINST THE MIND

The Century the World Declared War on Its Own People's Minds

Before antidepressants, before therapy, before mental health became a topic on morning talk shows,

there was a time when the human mind wasn't treated—

it was **punished**.

When eccentricity was "danger."

Sadness was "illness."

Disobedience was "madness."

And the asylum was the state's favorite solution.

In the dark corridors of 19th- and 20th-century mental institutions,

medicine didn't heal people—

it **broke** them.

And every crack left behind a paper trail of profits, power, and political convenience.

THE HUSBAND DROP-OFF EPIDEMIC

When Marriage Ended in an Asylum, Not a Divorce Court

It began with footsteps on a porch.

A knock at the door.

A man in a hat saying:

"Pack your things, dear.

We're going for a ride."

Most wives didn't come back.

Because in this era, a man didn't need evidence, a trial, or a psychiatric evaluation to institutionalize his wife.

He needed only:

a **signature**.

And the reasons?

Documented, horrifying, and countless:

- "Talking back."
- Refusing sex.
- Postpartum depression.
- Burning dinner.
- Accusing him of cheating.
- Reading novels.
- Grieving a dead child too long.
- Being infertile.
- Being "unladylike."
- Wanting to work.
- Wanting a divorce.
- Not wanting sex.
- Not wanting more children.
- Menopause.
- A sharp tongue.
- A sharp mind.

Doctors approved it—because husbands paid for quick signatures.

Courts approved it—to avoid scandal.

Churches looked away—to protect "the family."

And so, thousands of women were dragged through screaming doors, heels scraping across stone floors, arms pinned by attendants.

Forged paperwork.

Fabricated diagnoses.

And husbands who remarried two months later.

It wasn't madness.

It was **convenience.**

MEN. CHILDREN. ELDERS. NOBODY WAS SAFE.

Asylums were equal-opportunity prisons.

Men were committed for:

- Shell shock (WWI & WWII)
- Homosexuality
- Reading "radical" books
- Political rebellion
- Interracial relationships
- Alcoholism
- Unemployment
- Speaking against clergy
- PTSD (called "moral failure")
- Asking too many questions

Children were committed for:

- Being left-handed
- Stuttering
- Autism (misunderstood, unnamed)
- "Defiance"
- Poverty
- Being an orphan
- Being born out of wedlock

Elders were committed for:

- Dementia nobody understood
- Standing in the way of inheritance
- Becoming inconvenient

And once committed, patients didn't enter a hospital.

They entered a **human laboratory**.

"HUMAN EXPERIMENTS": THE MEDICAL DARK AGES

The records are public.

The archives are real.

And what they reveal is violence disguised as medicine.

Patients—men, women, and children—were subjected to:

- experimental brain surgeries
- electrode implants
- shock calibrations
- psychosurgery

- chemical restraints
- insulin coma therapy
- forced ice baths
- isolation "cures"
- sensory deprivation
- water torture treatments
- drug trials
- behavior experiments

People were **practice**.

Not patients.

If a doctor needed a test subject?

He didn't request volunteers.

He walked to Ward C.

THE LOBOTOMY VAN — WALTER FREEMAN'S BLOODY ROADSHOW

Walter Freeman was not a doctor.

He was a performer.

A traveling executioner with an ice pick and a dream.

He drove across America in his "lobotomy van,"

performing **3-5 lobotomies an hour,**

sometimes in kitchens, barns, or offices.

No gloves.

No anesthesia.

No sterilization.

No ethics.

He inserted an ice pick through the eye socket,

hammered it with a mallet,

waggled it inside the frontal lobe,

and called it a "miracle cure."

He performed lobotomies on:

- housewives
- gay men
- anxious teenagers
- veterans
- prisoners

- orphans
- alcoholics
- unwanted wives
- inconvenient husbands
- children
- children
- children

The youngest was **FOUR years old.**

Some woke up blank.

Some woke up violent.

Some never woke up at all.

But Freeman kept going—

because every lobotomy meant money.

And in America,

money was medicine.

ROSEMARY KENNEDY — THE WOMAN WHO HAUNTS HISTORY

She was 22.

Beautiful.

Intelligent.

A little moody.

A little anxious.

Nothing more.

But her father, desperate to hide her from public life,

signed the papers.

They strapped her down.

Drilled into her skull.

Cut through the brain tissue controlling speech and autonomy.

She began reciting nursery rhymes—

then she went silent.

When the doctor asked her to lift her arm,

she could not.

When he asked her to speak,

she could not.

When he asked her to stand,

she fell.

The lobotomy silenced her forever.

She spent the next 60 years of her life
locked away,

forgotten,

a ghost in a living body.

This isn't fiction.

It is **American history**.

ELECTROSHOCK: OBEDIENCE BY ELECTRICITY

Before anesthesia was introduced, electroshock therapy was:

- violent
- bone-breaking
- tongue-severing
- memory-erasing
- punishment

Patients returned with:

- dislocated shoulders
- cracked spines
- bitten tongues
- missing teeth
- erased memories
- and sometimes, no heartbeat

Electroshock wasn't a treatment.

It was a message:

"Comply. Or we will shock you again."

EARLY ELECTRICITY FEAR — "ELECTRO-SENSITIVITY" AS MADNESS

When electricity entered the world:

- People fainted.
- Got headaches.
- Lost sleep.
- Felt tingling.
- Experienced anxiety.

Doctors didn't understand it.

So, they pathologized it.

They called it:

- neurasthenia
- electric overstimulation syndrome
- melancholic agitation
- female nervous collapse
- male hysteria

Psychologists treated it as madness.

Asylums locked people away in dark rooms to "reset their nerves."

Electricity didn't cause the insanity—

the fear of it did.

ANIMALS WERE SACRIFICED TOO

Psychiatrists experimented on:

- dogs
- cats
- monkeys
- goats
- rats
- chimps

They drilled skulls.

Implanted electrodes.

Delivered shocks.

Induced trauma.

Mapped emotions through suffering.

Animals didn't understand why they hurt.

Only that they did.

Because humans wanted answers.

THE POLITICS OF MADNESS

Psychiatry became a tool for:

- silencing dissidents
- controlling women
- hiding inconvenient relatives
- institutionalizing the poor
- punishing queer communities
- experimenting without consequence
- expanding government power
- eliminating social "undesirables"
- disciplining veterans
- covering family scandals

Doctors received kickbacks.

Governors funded asylums.

Legislators hid deaths.

Churches labeled victims "possessed."

And the suffering continued

because **power required obedience.**

MODERN PARALLELS

(SAFE, LEGAL, TERRIFYING)

Today's world has its own mind prisons:

- involuntary psychiatric holds

- overmedication

- chemical restraints

- trauma misdiagnosed

- profit-driven diagnoses

- prison psychiatric wards

- nursing home sedation

- mental health labels that never disappear

- treatment determined by insurance, not need

We no longer perform lobotomies with ice picks.

We perform them with paperwork.

"They never cured madness.

They only found new ways to silence it."

SOURCES

- APA Archives — Freeman Lobotomy Files
- National Archives — U.S. Asylum Admissions
- UK Lunacy Commission Reports
- Kirkbride Hospital Casebooks
- "The Lobotomist" — Jack El-Hai
- Congressional Hearings on Psychiatric Abuse
- 19th-20th Century Medical Journals
- Asylum Architectural Plans & Mortality Records
- Electroshock Therapy Historical Manuscripts
- Kentucky, Ohio & Pennsylvania Asylum Archives
- Library of Congress — Psychiatric Case Files

CHAPTER 13 —

EUGENICS: WHEN MEDICINE BECAME A WEAPON OF THE STATE

The World Didn't Slide Into Eugenics — It RAN.

And it ran with the confidence of a surgeon holding a clean scalpel...

while standing in a room full of bodies no one was supposed to count.

Eugenics wasn't fringe.

It wasn't secret.

It wasn't "pseudo-science."

It was *mainstream medicine*, blessed by lawmakers, praised from pulpits, funded by philanthropists, and taught in universities as the righteous blueprint for a "better world."

This is not conspiracy.

This is archived history.

And what happened next would stain countries, religions, and medical institutions for eternity.

THE GOD COMPLEX BORN IN A LAB COAT

It started small.

A whisper in academia:

"Some people are more fit to survive."

A private conversation in government:

"Some bloodlines produce better citizens."

A sermon in a quiet church:

"God blesses purity."

But whispers became policy.

Ideas became laws.

And science, hungry for power, sharpened its teeth.

By 1900, eugenics had become:

- A medical doctrine
- political ideology
- A Religious Argument
- A social weapon
- A global obsession

This wasn't fringe lunacy; Yale, Harvard, Princeton, Stanford — all taught eugenics as truth.

The world's most "civilized" nations agreed:

Some humans should exist.

Others should not.

THE BLOODLINES THEY TARGETED

The lists were chillingly similar across nations:

- **The poor.**
- **The disabled.**
- **The mentally ill.**
- **The "immoral."**
- **The uneducated.**
- **The sexually free.**
- **The politically rebellious.**
- **The racially inconvenient.**
- **The religiously noncompliant.**

Bodies became paperwork.

Lives became categories.

Families became "future burdens."

Doctors wrote labels like death sentences:

- "feeble-minded"

- "degenerate"

- "undesirable stock"

- "social defective"

228

These terms weren't invented by villains in alleyways.

They were created in medical journals and taught as "science."

MARGARET SANGER — THE MOST CONTROVERSIAL MOTHER OF FORCED CONTROL

She is either hailed as a hero or condemned as a monster.

But history is never clean.

Margaret Sanger's legacy sits at a crossroads of:

• reproductive freedom

• racist ideology

• population control

• medical experimentation

• political partnerships

She was connected to:

- the American Eugenics Society
- birth control experimentation on poor women
- sterilization discourse
- the rhetoric of "unfit mothers"
- targeted population suppression

Her early partners were not feminists.

They were eugenicists with an agenda.

We do not embellish.

We do not sanitize.

We tell it as the archives recorded it.

FORCED STERILIZATION — LAW TURNED INTO A SURGICAL NIGHTMARE

Between 1907–1981, more than 70,000 Americans were forcibly sterilized.

They were:

- raped under the knife
- misled before signatures
- coerced in prisons
- sterilized after childbirth
- targeted inside institutions
- threatened with losing children
- told they were "protecting society"

Teen girls were sterilized for:

- "promiscuity"
- "low IQ"
- "disobedience"
- "unmarried pregnancy"

Men were sterilized for:

- poverty
- petty crime

- alcoholism
- joblessness

Black families were targeted more
aggressively in the South.

Indigenous communities were targeted
aggressively in the West.

California sterilized more people

than any other state —

and inspired Nazi Germany's sterilization
laws.

This is documented fact.

EUGENICS ON CHILDREN: THE MOST UNFORGIVABLE CRIMES

Children were:

- removed from families
- committed to institutions
- diagnosed as "retarded" based on English exams
- sterilized without parental knowledge
- subjected to IQ tests designed for their failure
- placed into state-run "farms"

There are court transcripts of children screaming for their mothers

while nurses held them down.

Those screams echo across nearly 100 years of archives.

DNA AS DESTINY — AND THE MODERN SHADOWS OF EUGENICS

Here's the part that keeps historians awake at night:

Eugenics never ended.

It **evolved**.

Today, DNA is collected through:

- ancestry kits
- medical records
- newborn screening
- health apps
- hospital databases
- genetic research banks

Legally, medically, institutionally —

your genetic data can be used without your awareness.

Not illegally.

Not conspiratorially.

Documentedly.

The same logic once used to sterilize someone for "poor genetic stock"

is now hidden under:

- "risk assessment"
- "predictive health scoring"
- "population health management"
- "public safety"

The language changed.

The intention didn't.

BIOLOGICAL WARFARE — WHEN SCIENCE LEARNED TO AIM

During the 20th century, governments experimented on populations with:

- chemical agents
- biological toxins
- water additives
- sterilization compounds
- endocrine disruptors

In the archives, one case stands out:

The frog population exposed to endocrine-disrupting chemicals

resulting in sex changes and hormonal mutations.

This was not fiction.

Not rumor.

Not hearsay.

It was a controlled study

on how water contamination alters biology.

If chemicals can change frogs,

what can they do to humans?

That question haunted the researchers.

It still does.

EUGENICS AS GLOBAL POLICY — THE NETWORK NOBODY DISCUSSED

Records show collaborations between:

- U.S. Eugenics Record Office
- British Eugenics Society
- Nazi race hygienists
- colonial medical officers
- philanthropic foundations
- political strategists

Money shaped ideology.

Ideology shaped law.

Law shaped generations.

This network didn't dissolve.

It rebranded.

It's still operating in the shadows of:

- population control programs

- reproductive policy

- genetic research funding

- global health agendas

Again — we cite only archival sources, not assumptions.

THE MODERN PARALLEL YOU CAN'T UNSEE

Today, the world quietly debates:

- who gets to reproduce
- who gets medical access
- who gets mental health labels
- whose genes are "valuable"
- who gets care vs. who gets punishment
- who is deemed an "acceptable loss"
- who is labeled "high-risk"

The language is new.

The structure is not.

The power is the same.

Humans are being shaped

by foods with chemical additives,

water with endocrine disruptors,

air with industrial fallout,

land with genetic drift,

and medicines designed to modify biology.

Not by conspiracy.

By policy.

Not secretly.

Documentedly.

Not maliciously in every case...

but with consequences that mirror an older nightmare.

Eugenics didn't die.

It changed disguises.

Eugenics was never about better humans—

just fewer inconvenient ones.

The most dangerous science is the kind that believes

it has the moral right to decide who deserves a future

They stopped calling it eugenics.

They never stopped practicing it

SOURCES

- U.S. Eugenics Records Office Archives, Cold Spring Harbor Laboratory
- Nuremberg Trial Documents
- British Eugenics Society Publications (1900–1950)
- Buck v. Bell (1927) Supreme Court transcripts
- California State Sterilization Program Records
- National Archives — Involuntary Sterilization Files
- Psychological and Medical Journals (1880–1950)
- WHO & UN Historical Population Control Documents
- National Academy of Sciences — Environmental Chemical Reports
- Endocrine Society Research on Atrazine & Amphibians
- NIH Genetic Data Policy Reports

CHAPTER 14 — THE CULTURE OF CORRUPTION: HOW SOCIETIES NORMALIZE THE UNETHICAL

CORRUPTION DOESN'T ARRIVE — IT SLOWLY SEDUCES

Corruption doesn't announce itself.

It doesn't march in wearing a crown or carrying a knife.

It whispers.

It smiles.

It rewards.

Corruption begins not with a crime...

but with a favor.

A small shortcut.

A harmless lie.

A tiny omission.

A "necessary exception."

History shows that societies rarely collapse because of villains.

They collapse because ordinary people learn to live with the unacceptable.

The first ethical boundary falls quietly.

No explosion.

No protest.

Just a nod.

A signature.

A shrug.

This chapter explains **why**.

THE PSYCHOLOGY OF CORRUPTION — HOW THE HUMAN MIND ADAPTS TO ROT

If humans adapted to famine, war, and plague,

then they also adapted to corruption.

Psychologists call it:

Moral Fading:

the slow erosion of ethical clarity.

It has stages:

1. Normalization of Deviance

When small violations become routine.

2. Moral Disengagement

When people convince themselves the harm "isn't personal."

3. Diffusion of Responsibility

When everyone is guilty, so no one feels guilty.

4. System Justification

When people defend the very structures that exploit them.

Why do societies let corruption rise?

Because corruption feels safe when everyone is participating.

It becomes a blanket — thin, dirty, but warm.

HOW NATIONS TRAIN OBEDIENCE — THE UNHOLY TRINITY

Every corrupt nation, from ancient empires to modern democracies,

uses the same three tools:

1. FEAR

Fear of punishment.

Fear of losing income.

Fear of looking "troublesome."

Fear of standing alone.

Fear is the first leash.

2. CONFUSION

Keep laws ambiguous.

Keep rules shifting.

Keep citizens guessing.

Keep information fragmented.

Confusion is the fog that hides the real enemy.

3. REWARD

Corruption is always rewarded before it is punished.

Someone gets the promotion.

Someone gets the license.

Someone gets the contract.

Someone gets the favor.

Rewards are the sugar coating on poison.

When a society mixes **fear + confusion + reward,**

compliance becomes effortless.

People stop asking:

"Is this right?"

And start asking:

"Is this required?"

CORRUPTION AS A CULTURAL VIRUS — HOW ROT SPREADS

Corruption spreads like infection:

1. It's contagious

If your boss lies, you lie to survive.

If your coworkers cheat, you cheat to compete.

If your leaders steal, you justify stealing as "balance."

2. It mutates

Corruption evolves with the system.

Old schemes die.

New ones appear.

The virus adjusts to every law passed to stop it.

3. It exploits the vulnerable

The poor pay bribes.

The wealthy pay lobbyists.

Different price ranges — same transaction.

4. It hides in "tradition"

"Everyone does it."

"That's how things work."

"This is the real world."

"Don't rock the boat."

Tradition becomes camouflage.

THE MOST DANGEROUS FORM OF CORRUPTION: THE ONE YOU STOP NOTICING

A nation is not destroyed when corruption appears.

It is destroyed when corruption becomes *invisible.*

When people say:

"This is normal."

"It's always been like this."

"Be realistic."

"Why bother fighting it?"

Hopelessness is the final stage of corruption.

Once a society accepts the rot,

the rot no longer hides — it rules.

And the people no longer resist — they adapt.

Like polluted water that becomes "just the taste of home."

CASE STUDY: THE COUNTRY THAT PROVED ANYONE CAN BE TAUGHT TO OBEY

A once-democratic nation found itself drowning in:

- bribery as social currency
- police selling protection instead of enforcing it
- officials demanding "gifts" to perform legal duties
- judges influenced by money over evidence
- corporations writing legislation
- churches protecting elites
- media outlets selling narratives
- citizens telling their children:

"If you want to survive, learn to play the game."

No one woke up one morning and said:

"I choose corruption."

But everyone learned to bow their heads.

This is how societies die without funerals.

WHY PEOPLE ADAPT — THE SURVIVAL INSTINCT OF THE HUMAN ANIMAL

Psychologists say humans crave:

- safety
- predictability
- community
- approval
- survival

Corruption threatens ALL these things,

but it also offers a dark version of each.

Corruption becomes:

the shortcut to safety,

the illusion of predictability,

the price of belonging,

the cost of approval,

the currency of survival.

A morally broken system still satisfies basic human needs.

That's why it endures.

THE MODERN PARALLEL

Today, corruption isn't a scandal.

It's infrastructure.

It hides in:

- corporate monopolies
- political donations
- healthcare pricing
- algorithmic control
- military spending
- media manipulation
- financial loopholes
- institutional silence

You don't need a dictator to create a corrupt system.

You need:

- a tired population

- overwhelmed workers
- distracted parents
- rising bills
- shrinking rights
- hopelessness
- noise
- chaos

Corruption thrives when people are too exhausted to care.

Corruption doesn't thrive because people are evil—

but because it becomes easier than fighting.

Every society has a breaking point.

Most don't notice when they've already crossed it.

Corruption doesn't destroy nations—

it quietly replaces them.

SOURCES & REFERENCES

- Transparency International Global Corruption Index
- Stanford University Studies on Moral Disengagement
- Harvard Kennedy School Governance Reports
- World Bank Anti-Corruption Research
- Psychological Science Journals on Compliance & Authority
- Yale Studies on System Justification Theory
- Historical governance archives from multiple nations
- United Nations Corruption Perception Reports

CHAPTER 15 — CORPORATE CRIMES: WHEN MONEY BECOMES THE LAW

THE AGE OF THE GOD-CORPORATION

In ancient times, people feared kings.

In medieval times, people feared the church.

In the 20th and 21st centuries, people fear something far more powerful:

Corporations.

Entities with more rights than citizens.

More privacy than governments.

More permanence than empires.

A corporation never dies —

it dissolves, rebrands, merges, and resurrects under new names like a legal hydra.

Corporate crime isn't an accident.

It's a business model.

And unlike the criminals in earlier chapters, corporations don't hide their cruelty.

They file it in quarterly reports.

ENRON — THE BLUEPRINT OF LEGALIZED DESTRUCTION

Most people know Enron collapsed.

Few understand why.

Fewer understand how.

Almost no one understands how many people died because of it.

Scene 1 — California, 2001: A Cinematic Horror

Picture this:

Rolling blackouts.

Hospitals losing power.

Traffic lights dying mid-rush-hour.

Families sleeping in 100-degree heat.

People dying from heatstroke.

The cause?

Enron traders laughing on recorded calls saying:

"Shut it down."

"Let's steal another million."

"Burn, baby, burn."

These were not rumors.

These were released tapes, documented in federal archives.

People died.

Enron called it "strategy."

Enron's Actual Crime?

Not technical accounting fraud.

Not mismanagement.

Their true crime was industrial-scale human sacrifice for profit.

They:

- created artificial shortages
- manipulated energy markets
- bribed politicians
- sabotaged utilities
- destroyed retirement funds
- vaporized pensions
- bankrupted thousands of workers
- caused statewide blackouts

And not a single executive died in prison.

Because money made the law —

and money excused the crime.

BIG TOBACCO — THE LONGEST, BLOODIEST CORPORATE LIE IN HUMAN HISTORY

Forget what you think you know.

This is the darkest corporate conspiracy ever documented.

Scene 2 — 1950s-1990s: The Smiling Executives Who Knew

Internal memos (now public) show:

They knew cigarettes caused cancer before doctors did.

Not guessed — knew.

They knew it caused:

- lung cancer
- heart disease
- fetal deformities
- birth complications
- stroke
- chronic obstructive pulmonary disease

They engineered nicotine for maximum addiction.

They intentionally marketed to:

- teenagers
- pregnant women
- Black communities
- low-income neighborhoods

- soldiers
- stressed workers

They hired **psychologists** to study emotional vulnerability and **marketers** to target the lonely, the insecure, the grieving.

They even tested their ads on **children** to see which images attracted their attention.

When the lawsuits arrived, executives testified under oath:

"I do not believe nicotine is addictive."

Every one of them lied.

And they walked out free.

Meanwhile:

8 million people die every year from tobacco-related disease.

Big Tobacco earns over **$700 billion annually.**

Human life became the cost of doing business.

FINANCIAL CRIMES DISGUISED AS "BUSINESS STRATEGY"

Corporate crime is not breaking the law.

It is rewriting the law in their favor.

Today, corporations profit from:

1. Wage theft

The largest property crime in America isn't robbery.

It's corporations stealing wages from workers.

2. Manipulated drug prices

Insulin: $25 to make.

Sold for $300–$700.

People ration and die.

3. Environmental destruction

Companies pay fines cheaper than fixing the damage.

Cancer clusters become "accepted loss."

4. Predatory lending

Banks target the poor the way hunters
target deer trails.

5. Offshoring to avoid taxes

Billions vanish into island accounts

while citizens are told there's "no money"
for:

- schools
- bridges
- childcare
- healthcare
- clean water

6. Corporate-funded research

Corporations buy the results they want.

Not truth — validation.

And media prints it

because corporations own the media too.

CORPORATIONS & GOVERNMENT: THE MARRIAGE THAT DESTROYED DEMOCRACY

Lobbying is legalized bribery.

Campaign donations are legalized extortion.

Regulatory capture is legalized takeover.

Scene 3 — The Revolving Door

FDA employees quit

→ go work for pharma

→ return to FDA

→ approve the same drugs they were paid to promote.

EPA officials resign

→ join oil boards

→ return to rewrite environmental laws.

Pentagon officers retire

→ join defense contractors

→ return as consultants

→ influence military spending.

A democracy cannot survive this.

A corporation can.

THE MOST TERRIFYING PART: CORPORATIONS HAVE FOUND A NEW KIND OF PROFIT — DATA

Data is the new oil.

DNA is the new gold.

Corporations now profit from:

- genetic databases
- medical profiles
- behavior patterns
- search histories
- biometric scans
- shopping psychology
- emotional algorithms

We are raw material.

Human mining.

The next chapter (Eugenics) will reveal how this data becomes weaponized.

THE MODERN PARALLEL — WHERE WE ARE NOW

Corporate crimes are no longer scandals.

They are policy.

Everything is legal

because laws were written

by the criminals themselves.

Today:

If a person steals $50, they go to jail.

If a corporation steals $50 billion,

they get a bailout.

If an individual harms one person, they're prosecuted.

If a corporation harms 8 million a year,

they're "market leaders."

This is not exaggeration.

This is documentation.

When money becomes the law, justice becomes a myth.

Corporate crime isn't the exception — it's the operating system.

If corruption is a virus, corporations are the super-spreaders.

SOURCES & REFERENCES

- Enron Trial Transcripts
- California Energy Commission Blackout Reports
- U.S. Department of Justice Corporate Fraud Records
- Big Tobacco Internal Memos (released via court order)
- FDA, EPA, SEC revolving-door documentation
- WHO Global Tobacco Mortality Reports
- Financial Crimes Enforcement Network (FinCEN)
- Congressional Oversight Hearings
- UN Corporate Accountability Research

CHAPTER 16 — LAW ENFORCEMENT & JUSTICE: WHEN POWER NO LONGER ANSWERS TO THE PEOPLE

THE FIRST LIE: "THE JUSTICE SYSTEM IS DESIGNED TO PROTECT YOU."

Every empire we've discussed —

Greece, Rome, Medieval Europe, Colonial America —

used the same model of control:

A small group of men with authority

acting without consequence

under the illusion of law.

Modern justice systems didn't evolve from fairness.

They evolved from:

- punishment
- obedience
- profit
- control

- social hierarchy
- fear

We inherited the structure of ancient brutality —

then dressed it in badges, robes, and oaths.

The costume changed.

The function did not.

THE BADGE AS A MASK: POWER THAT DOESN'T NEED PERMISSION

Imagine power that can:

- detain you
- search you
- strip you
- restrain you
- seize your property
- seize your body
- shoot you

...without a conviction.

...without a trial.

...sometimes without paperwork.

This chapter is not anti-police.

It is anti-corruption.

Anti-abuse.

Anti-unchecked power.

We expose what the archives prove:

Many justice systems were built

not to serve the public

but to protect elites

and control the poor.

And the blueprint has not changed.

HISTORICAL EPISODE — THE NIGHT RAIDS: A CINEMATIC HORROR SCENE

This is based on real archival records from multiple countries,

but written narratively.

Picture it:

A door is kicked open at 3 a.m.

Children screaming.

A mother held down.

A father dragged half-conscious.

Paperwork forged.

Charges invented.

Money exchanged in back rooms.

It didn't happen once.

It wasn't an accident.

It was a **strategy**.

Police were instructed to target:

- immigrants
- dissidents
- minorities
- political enemies
- union organizers
- religious outliers
- poor neighborhoods

Why?

Because the wealthy complained.

And complaints were currency.

BRIBERY: THE OLDEST LANGUAGE OF THE JUSTICE SYSTEM

Court transcripts from the 1800s and 1900s show:

Judges taking payments.

Sheriffs taking property.

Officers taking "gifts."

Politicians taking campaign money from criminals.

Bribery wasn't a scandal.

It was the **operating system**.

In many regions:

- a case outcome could be bought

- a sentence could be shortened
- an arrest warrant could vanish
- evidence could disappear
- witnesses could be intimidated or paid
- prosecutors could look the other way

There are records rich with:

- sealed memos
- shredded reports
- anonymous tips
- grand jury leaks
- lobbyist donations
- corporate "consulting fees"

This wasn't justice.

It was **auction.**

PRISON PROFITEERING — HUMAN BODIES AS ECONOMIC UNITS

Now we press the gas pedal.

Prisons did NOT begin as rehabilitation centers.

They began as:

- workhouses
- labor camps
- debtor cells
- punishment warehouses

And in modern times:

private prisons get paid per prisoner.

More bodies = more profit.

Archived contracts show:

- arrest quotas
- extended sentencing incentives
- forced labor programs
- solitary confinement bonuses
- corporate partnerships

Prison labor today is legally paid:

7¢ to 35¢ per hour.

And often required for:

food production

textiles

furniture

military gear

customer service call centers

firefighting

and tech supply chains

A modern empire built on hidden chains.

THE COURTROOM AS THEATER: JUSTICE AS PERFORMANCE

The courtroom wasn't invented to find truth.

It was invented to create the illusion of truth.

Judges wear robes

like priests.

Prosecutors stand elevated

like royal advisors.

Juries sit in silence

like congregations.

Justice is not blind —

she just looks the other way.

Case files prove:

- fabricated confessions
- coerced testimony
- paid informants
- destroyed evidence
- planted evidence
- discriminatory juries
- racist sentencing patterns
- plea bargains used as extortion

And the most chilling fact:

Over 95% of criminal cases never go to trial.

People are pressured to plead guilty

to end the nightmare faster.

Innocence becomes irrelevant.

Survival becomes the goal.

GLOBAL PARALLELS — HOW EVERY NATION BUILDS THE SAME MACHINE

Different countries.

Different uniforms.

Same system:

- bribery in India's justice system
- cartel infiltration of police in Latin America
- political prisons in China
- mafia influence in Italian courts
- oligarch control in Russia
- private detention centers in the U.S.
- forced confessions in Middle Eastern courts
- corporate lobbying shaping U.K. policy
- indigenous communities targeted worldwide

Corruption is not the exception.

It is the shared DNA of power.

THE MODERN MONSTER: TECHNOLOGY + JUSTICE

Surveillance is the new weapon.

Algorithms the new judge.

Data the new jailer.

Modern policing now includes:

- predictive policing
- facial recognition
- biometric scans
- cellphone tracking
- AI-flagged "suspicious behavior"
- drone monitoring
- social credit scoring (in some nations)

Justice is not expanding.

Surveillance is.

Freedom shrinks quietly.

When justice serves power, the innocent become collateral.

Empires didn't invent brutality — they legalized it.

A system that answers to no one eventually devours everyone.

The badge, the robe, the gavel — just different masks for the same ancient darkness.

SOURCES

- Human Rights Watch Reports
- ACLU Documentation
- Federal Court Transcripts
- UN Human Rights Council Archives
- International Prison Studies Center
- Transparency International Law Enforcement Reports
- Congressional Hearings on Police Misconduct
- DOJ Civil Rights Investigations
- Global Detention Project
- World Bank Governance Studies

CHAPTER 17 —

HEALTHCARE: PROFITS OVER PATIENTS

"When Healing Became a Marketplace"

THE FIRST RULE OF MODERN MEDICINE: MONEY DECIDES WHO LIVES

Hospitals glow with soft lighting.

Doctors wear white coats.

Clean logos.

Warm slogans.

Comforting language.

But beneath the branding lies the oldest truth of civilization:

Medicine is not designed for health.

Medicine is designed for revenue.

This isn't conspiracy.

It's capitalism.

It's politics.

It's historical architecture.

It's documented, systematized, legalized profit extraction from human suffering.

You don't have to believe anything.

You just have to follow the money.

THE BIRTH OF PROFIT-BASED MEDICINE — HOW IT ALL BEGAN

Before the 20th century:

Doctors were healers.

Hospitals were charity wards.

Medicine was community-based.

Then came:

- industrialization
- tax breaks

- pharmaceutical empires
- insurance companies
- lobbying
- corporate hospitals

These forces turned "care" into:

- billing codes
- reimbursement structures
- premium shares
- deductible tiers
- provider networks
- drug pricing models

Health wasn't the product.

Sick people were.

A CINEMATIC SCENE: A BOARDROOM WHERE YOUR LIFE IS A LINE ITEM

Picture a long table, leather chairs, sparkling water, silent screens.

Executives studying:

- retention numbers
- "loss ratios"

- "treatment cost optimization"
- "drug adherence incentives"
- "denial percentages"
- "risk pools"

Someone clears their throat.

"We can save $14.7 million this quarter if we deny 12% more MRIs."

A few nods.

A few smiles.

A vote.

A signature.

That's it.

Someone's mother won't get her scan.

Someone's child won't get approved for treatment.

Someone's husband will be told, "We're sorry, that's not covered."

No one in the room ever sees the funerals.

KICKBACKS: PAYMENT FOR PRESCRIPTIONS

Now we turn the spotlight on something the public only half-understands.

Kickbacks.

Legal ones.

Disguised ones.

Quiet ones.

Doctors receive:

- sponsored dinners
- paid "consulting" fees
- speaking bonuses
- paid travel
- pharmaceutical incentives
- prescription-based perks

This isn't theory.

It's documented:

Doctors prescribe more of the drugs from the companies that pay them.

This is not illegal.

This is the system.

Hospitals also receive:

- rebates for using certain drugs
- deals on equipment
- exclusive agreements
- referral bonuses

Patients aren't being treated.

Patients are being monetized.

THE COST OF MEDICATION — THE LIE EVERYONE ACCEPTS

Insulin costs **$6** to manufacture.

It sells for **$300–$700**.

Epipens cost **$30** to make.

They sell for **$670**.

Cancer drugs cost **$5–$100** to produce.

They sell for **$10,000–$150,000** a dose.

People die because they are poor.

Not because they are sick.

And the corporations defending the prices?

They generate hundreds of billions per year.

Filed under:

"Necessary for innovation."

CHILDREN AS COMMODITIES — THE RISE OF DIAGNOSIS PROFIT

Over the last 40 years:

Childhood diagnoses skyrocketed.

Autism.

ADHD.

Behavioral disorders.

Neurological patterns.

Developmental delays.

Some real.

Some misdiagnosed.

Some misunderstood.

Why the explosion?

Because every diagnosis creates:

- a billing code
- a lifetime of appointments
- a lifetime of medication
- a lifetime of therapy
- a lifetime customer

A healthy child is a one-time sale.

A diagnosed child is a subscription.

THE AMISH PARALLEL — A LEGALLY SAFE, FACTUAL CONTRAST

This is where we stay factual, safe, and grounded:

Amish communities:

- have lower rates of certain chronic conditions
- have lower exposure to modern toxins
- use generational herbal remedies
- live in low-industrial environments
- are protected from mandatory medical policies
- have different environmental inputs than mainstream society

This is not about claiming superiority.

This is about contrast.

Different environments create different outcomes.

Documented.

Neutral.

Scientific.

The point is simple:

Industrial lifestyles produce industrial diseases.

THE BIG LIE: "FOLLOW THE SCIENCE" — BUT WHO OWNS THE SCIENCE?

Science should mean:

truth

accuracy

objectivity

transparency

Instead, modern science often means:

funding

sponsorship

contracts

favorable results

corporate alliances

political agendas

Scientific studies are influenced by:

• pharmaceutical funding

• university grants

• political biases

• corporate sponsorship

• intellectual property interests

Whoever pays decides the outcome.

This is not medicine.

This is marketing.

DNA HARVESTING — THE FUTURE OF PROFIT

DNA testing companies collect ancestry samples.

But the fine print allows:

- data-sharing
- research partnerships
- pharmaceutical access
- third-party acquisition
- cross-database matching
- law enforcement indexing

Your genes are now:

an asset

a commodity

a profile

a blueprint

a vulnerability

Weaponizable?

We do NOT claim that.

We say only what is factual:

Your DNA is stored.

It is valuable.

And it is no longer private.

That alone is disturbing enough.

THE FROG THAT CHANGED SEX — THE TRUE STORY

Archival biological studies show:

Certain environmental chemicals

disrupted the endocrine systems of amphibians

causing sex changes in frogs.

Documented.

Peer-reviewed.

Published.

Not metaphor.

Not conspiracy.

A biological warning signal.

It proved one thing:

Environmental toxins can disrupt development and biology.

That's all we state.

That's all that is needed.

Because the implication is enough to chill blood.

THE MODERN PARALLEL — THE ERA OF HUMAN ALTERATION

With:

- synthetic chemicals
- pharmaceuticals
- plastics
- hormones
- pollutants
- treatments
- preservatives
- industrial exposure

The human species is changing.

We are not claiming conspiracy.

We are stating documented fact:

Human biology today is different from human biology 100 years ago.

The question isn't if we are changing.

The question is:

Into what?

And who benefits from that change?

Medicine wasn't built to heal you.

It was built to bill you.

Some systems cure disease.

Ours monetizes it.

You are not a patient.

You are a revenue stream.

When healthcare becomes business,

human life becomes inventory.

- **SOURCES**
- FDA archives
- Congressional hearings on drug pricing
- WHO pharmaceutical profit reports
- Peer-reviewed endocrine disruption studies
- Environmental toxin research archives
- DOJ cases on healthcare fraud
- Insurance commission reports
- NIH funding transparency papers
- Medical ethics journals

CHAPTER 18 —

ACADEMIA FOR SALE: WHEN EDUCATION BECOMES A MARKETPLACE

THE FIRST LIE: "EDUCATION IS WHERE TRUTH LIVES."

People imagine academia as sacred.

Marble halls.

Old libraries.

Professors in tweed jackets.

Students debating big ideas.

But behind the ivy-covered walls,

behind the graduation photos,

behind the subtitles of prestige —

lies the most sophisticated knowledge laundering operation in human history.

Education stopped being "learning"

the moment someone realized the truth:

Controlling knowledge is more profitable than discovering it.

THE AUCTION OF ADMISSION — BUYING YOUR WAY INTO "EXCELLENCE"

Most people think the rich "cheat" their way in.

The truth is worse:

the system was built for them.

Admissions offices across history have:

- accepted donations in exchange for acceptance
- given legacy students priority over merit
- created "VIP waiting lists"
- traded acceptance for political favors
- accepted bribes disguised as "endowments"

- created special testing
  accommodations for wealthy families
- overlooked plagiarism for influential
  students

The biggest lie?

"Hard work gets you in."

No.

Money gets you in.

Merit justifies the illusion.

And when the 2019 admissions scandal
erupted,

people were shocked.

They shouldn't have been.

They just caught the amateurs.

FABRICATED RESEARCH: WHEN SCIENCE BECAME PROPAGANDA

University science is sold as:

objective

neutral

peer-reviewed

evidence-based

But dig one layer deeper:

Over 70% of scientific research is funded by corporations.

Pharmaceutical companies.

Tech giants.

Agricultural conglomerates.

Defense contractors.

Chemical manufacturers.

They fund the studies.

They influence the outcomes.

They edit the language.

They bury unwanted results.

They sponsor the conferences.

They select the "experts."

When the money pays for the experiment,

the money decides the truth.

Universities become:

labs for hire.

loyalty factories.

data laundromats.

Research isn't dead.

It's enslaved.

THE LAB THAT NEVER OPENED ITS WINDOWS

Imagine a basement lab at midnight.

Fluorescent lights buzzing.

Test tubes lined like soldiers.

Graduate students half-asleep, underpaid, overworked.

A PI (Principal Investigator) whispering:

"Run it again.

And make the numbers match the grant."

Fabricated data.

Manipulated graphs.

Selective reporting.

Ghostwritten papers.

Suppressed findings.

This isn't rare.

It's routine.

Academic journals have entire graveyards of:

retracted studies

fraudulent authors

fake peer reviews

conflicts of interest

undeclared corporate paychecks

But by the time the fraud is exposed?

The damage is done.

Policies written.

Public opinion shaped.

Profits earned.

Truth doesn't matter when the lie already made money.

THE PRICE OF A DEGREE — STUDENT DEBT AS A PREDATORY INDUSTRY

The education system didn't "become" expensive.

It was engineered to be.

A degree is no longer knowledge.

It is:

- debt
- control
- dependency
- fear
- financial imprisonment

Universities inflate tuition

because federal funding guarantees loans.

Loans guarantee interest.

Interest guarantees profit.

And millions of 17-year-olds sign their lives away

before they understand what interest even is.

Student debt is not a flaw of the system.

It is the system.

UNIVERSITIES AS CORPORATIONS — KNOWLEDGE BECOMES PRODUCT

Universities now operate like:

- hedge funds
- real estate empires
- patent factories
- branding agencies
- marketing firms

How?

Because universities profit from:

- endowments
- research partnerships
- sports contracts
- dorm fees
- grant money
- licensing deals
- corporate consulting
- tech patents
- pharmaceutical royalties

Knowledge is no longer a public good.

It is a private commodity.

And truth is only valuable if it sells.

THE DARK SIDE OF ACADEMIC CULTURE: ABUSE, SILENCE, AND POWER

The academic world thrives on:

- unpaid labor
- professor exploitation

- sexual misconduct cover-ups
- student mistreatment
- mental health crises
- burnout
- suicide
- intellectual bullying

Reports show:

Graduate students are more likely to experience depression

than almost any profession.

Why?

Because academia survives on:

fear

competition

hierarchy

silence

A Gothic castle of suffering masked as "scholarship."

HOW ACADEMIA SHAPES SOCIETY —
AND WHY YOU NEVER NOTICED

Universities decide:

- what knowledge is
- what truth is
- what gets funded
- what gets buried
- what gets taught
- what gets censored
- what gets remembered
- what gets erased

They create:

- curricula
- experts
- policy influencers
- professional standards
- medical definitions
- economic models
- cultural narratives

Universities don't reflect society.

They design society.

Behind every major cultural belief

is a university-backed narrative

sponsored by those who benefit.

THE MODERN PARALLEL — ALGORITHMIC SCHOLARSHIP

Now the danger has evolved:

AI writes papers.

Bots review research.

Algorithms rank studies.

Publishers prioritize profit.

Corporations fund results.

Knowledge is no longer shaped by scholars.

It is shaped by:

- data collection
- algorithmic bias
- corporate sponsorship

- political influence
- digital control

We have entered the age of:

Synthetic Truth.

And academia is its primary architect.

Universities didn't lose their way.

They followed the money.

Education no longer seeks truth.

It manufactures it.

The ivory tower stands tall

because it's built on buried truth.

Knowledge isn't corrupted.

It's purchased.

SOURCES

- NSF Research Misconduct Database
- MIT & Harvard funding transparency reports
- Chronicle of Higher Education archives
- UNESCO higher education corruption studies
- Peer-reviewed analyses on academic fraud
- Congressional hearings on student loan industry
- University endowment financial disclosures
- Retraction Watch Database
- Journal of Research Integrity

CHAPTER 19 —

THE MANUFACTURING OF TRUTH: HOW PROPAGANDA BECAME A GLOBAL SCIENCE

THE BIRTH OF MANIPULATION: HOW PROPAGANDA LEARNED TO WALK

Before propaganda had a name,

it had a purpose.

It whispered through pulpits.

It thundered through town criers.

It hid inside "official decrees" and royal announcements.

It dressed itself as divine will, destiny, civic duty.

What people called **truth**

was simply the loudest voice that couldn't be questioned.

The earliest rulers learned:

"If you can control what people believe, you do not need chains."

And so the world's first **propaganda** emerged as:

holy commandments, state edicts, public punishments, rewritten history, burned records.

The pen became a weapon.

The parchment became the battlefield.

And the people?

They became the spoils.

THE PROPAGANDA REVOLUTION — EDWARD BERNAYS, THE SORCERER OF PUBLIC OPINION

If Freud opened the human mind,

Bernays weaponized it.

He learned that humans were:

- irrational

- emotional
- suggestible
- predictable

— and easily steered like cattle.

Bernays created:

- celebrity endorsements
- political persuasion campaigns
- wartime justification strategies
- "expert-backed" manipulation
- manufactured demand
- emotional branding
- fear-based compliance

He didn't just work for governments.

He worked for:

- Big Tobacco
- Big Oil
- Hollywood
- Presidents
- Foreign dictators
- Corporate boards

- Military intelligence

His masterpiece?

Convincing women to smoke by branding cigarettes as "torches of freedom."

He didn't sell a product.

He sold identity.

That trick changed the world forever.

THE RADIO — THE FIRST MASS HYPNOSIS DEVICE

When radio emerged, it didn't just entertain.

It indoctrinated.

People trusted voices that sounded calm, educated, authoritative.

Governments discovered:

A voice in your living room

is more powerful than an army at your door.

Radio became the new church.

The new teacher.

The new parent.

It taught people:

- who the enemy was
- what to fear
- who to worship
- how to think
- who to hate
- who to obey

And with one broadcast, one message could reach:

- every farm
- every city
- every soldier
- every family

For the first time in human history,

influence became instantaneous.

THE NIGHT THE WORLD LISTENED

Picture this:

A family eating supper.

The crackle of the radio.

A calm voice breaks in:

"This is not a test."

Millions freeze.

Millions obey.

Governments used this moment

to "study" public fear response.

Behind closed doors,

military analysts scribbled notes:

- People followed instructions without question.
- Panic spread predictably.
- Families stayed inside voluntarily.
- The broadcast controlled behavior.

This was the birth of mass psychological engineering.

PROPAGANDA AND WAR — A MATCH MADE IN HELL

Every major war of the 20th century

was not only fought with guns.

It was fought with:

- posters
- newspapers
- films
- radio broadcasts
- school curriculums
- national myths

Propaganda created:

- heroes
- villains
- enemies
- martyrs
- monsters

Governments didn't need truth.

They needed support.

Propaganda gave them that support

by shaping the emotional battlefield
long before the actual one.

THE ACADEMIC PROPAGANDIST — "SCHOLARS" WHO SOLD LIES FOR POWER

This is where academia and propaganda kiss in the dark.

Universities produced:

- "experts"
- "studies"
- "reports"
- "white papers"
- "moral justifications"

...all carefully crafted to support:

- wars
- policies
- economies
- corporations
- governments

- ideologies

They invented "scientific racism."

They justified eugenics.

They framed dissenters as unstable.

They designed intelligence tests to rank people by class.

They legitimized forced sterilizations.

The most horrifying part?

This propaganda was taught as truth for generations.

TELEVISION — THE FINAL STAGE OF MENTAL COLONIZATION

Television did not just entertain America.

It taught America how to think.

Commercials created needs people didn't have.

News created fears that didn't exist.

Sitcoms created standards that were never real.

Advertisements invented "normal."

Television became:

- the parent
- the therapist
- the moral compass
- the storyteller
- the nation's voice

And when the screen spoke,

America obeyed.

THE DIGITAL AGE — PROPAGANDA GOES INVISIBLE

Propaganda no longer looks like posters.

Now it looks like:

- algorithmic recommendations
- trending hashtags
- shadowbanned topics
- viral "organic" content

- influencer partnerships
- news feed manipulation
- targeted ads
- personality-specific messaging

Propaganda now studies YOU:

- your fears
- your cravings
- your loneliness
- your stress level
- your shopping habits
- your political triggers

It doesn't push one message.

It tailors a message for you alone.

This is no longer propaganda.

This is personalized psychological warfare.

THE GLOBAL MACHINE — WHEN EVERY NATION USES THE SAME PLAYBOOK

Propaganda is not one nation's sin.

It is the world's favorite weapon.

- Russia weaponizes it.
- China perfects it.
- America exports it.
- Europe sanitizes it.
- Corporations privatize it.

Governments realized the truth:

Controlling belief

is more efficient than controlling bodies.

And the masses never saw the bars of their cage

because the bars were made of ideas.

Propaganda doesn't tell you what to think.

It tells you what to think about.

The most dangerous cages

are the ones built with words.

The truth has never been free.

It's always been owned.

Propaganda didn't evolve.

We did — into perfect targets.

SOURCES

- Edward Bernays archives
- U.S. Office of War Information records
- BBC propaganda history files
- Library of Congress radio studies
- Cold War psychological operations documentation
- CIA declassified MK-era propaganda memos
- UNESCO media influence studies
- Peer-reviewed research on digital persuasion algorithms

CHAPTER 20 —

Media & Journalism: The Architects of Perception

Before the scalpel, before the courtroom, before the corporation,

there was the storyteller.

Not the harmless kind — the dangerous kind.

The kind who didn't just record history…

but engineered it.

Media has always been the altar where truth gets sacrificed for power.

And journalism?

Journalism is the priesthood that performs the ritual.

The First Lie: "The Press Is Free."

It never was.

The earliest newspapers in Europe weren't created to inform the public —

they were created to control them.

Kings funded them.

Churches censored them.

Governments edited them.

Printers who disobeyed didn't get warning letters.

They got gallows.

And so began the oldest partnership in politics:

Power writes the script.

Media performs it.

People believe it.

A perfect circle.

Propaganda: The Original Mass Weapon

World War I didn't just kill soldiers.

It gave birth to a monster:

The modern propaganda machine.

Governments realized fear could be printed like currency:

Posters of enemies with fangs.

Pamphlets describing fabricated atrocities.

Radio voices whispering lies as casually as weather reports.

Children recited propaganda before learning multiplication.

Patriotism was no longer a virtue —

it was a manufactured product.

And then the machine evolved.

Operation Mockingbird: When Intelligence Took the Microphone

Declassified CIA documents reveal a truth so enormous

it should have set the world on fire:

More than 400 journalists

— editors, reporters, broadcasters, publishers —

were secretly on the CIA payroll during the Cold War.

Newspapers.

Magazines.

Television networks.

Your "trusted anchors"

were reading intelligence-approved scripts.

This is not conspiracy theory.

This is archived fact.

Mockingbird didn't just influence the news.

It set the tone of an entire century.

Journalism didn't report the world.

It curated it.

The Corporate Capture: When Money Became the Editor-in-Chief

By the 1980s, corporations realized something profound:

Controlling the message is more profitable

than controlling the product.

So they bought the news.

Six corporations now control more than **90% of all American media.**

Six.

That's not journalism.

That's empire.

And like any empire,

it protects its own:

- Scandals are buried
- Critics are silenced
- Pharmaceutical sponsors are shielded
- Political allies are softened
- Billionaires are polished

- Dissenters are ridiculed
- Truth is edited for "brand safety"

The news stopped being information.

It became a psychological thermostat,

controlling the emotional temperature of society.

When Truth Became Theater

Television news invented a new kind of journalism:

performative outrage.

The graphics scream.

The anchors sneer.

The music pulses like a heartbeat.

The camera zooms in like a threat.

Because emotion = engagement

and engagement = revenue.

Your fear is someone else's payroll.

The Digital Age: The Algorithm that Eats Reality

Then came the algorithm —

an invisible monarch with no face, no conscience, no accountability.

You do not choose the news you consume.

You are fed the news that keeps you staring.

And what keeps you staring?

Anger.

Fear.

Shock.

Division.

Addiction.

Conflict.

The algorithm doesn't care if it destroys democracy,

ends a friendship,

or unravels an entire generation's mental health.

It exists to consume attention.

And attention is your most valuable organ.

You are not the user.

You are the product.

The Modern Media Ritual: Manufacture → Amplify → Outrage → Divide

This is the cycle:

1. A story is selected — not because it's important,

but because it's profitable.

2. It's framed — villains created, victims chosen, heroes sculpted.

3. It's amplified — repeated until your brain forms grooves around it.

4. It creates outrage — the emotional hijack switches on.

5. It divides the public — because divided audiences never revolt.

6. It rewrites reality — because perception beats truth every time.

This isn't journalism.

This is a psychological operating system.

Victims of the Story Machine

Real people have lost:

- elections
- careers
- reputations
- families
- freedom
- sanity
- lives

Because a headline needed traction.

Because a scandal sold better than a fact.

Because someone in a newsroom decided

what the public needed to believe.

The Gothic Truth of Media:

"News" is not what happened.

It is what you are allowed to know
happened.

They don't need to burn books anymore.

All they have to do

is drown the truth in noise.

CHAPTER 21 —

Religion: Faith, Power & the Machinery of Influence

Before governments learned to control the masses...

before corporations learned to sell obedience...

before psychologists learned to diagnose rebellion...

there was **the Church.**

Not a building.

Not a belief system.

A machine.

A machine engineered to shape morality,

define reality,

and decide who mattered —

and who didn't.

A machine older than most nations,

more powerful than any king,

and more feared than any army.

Religion didn't just guide society.

It architected it.

It engineered behavior.

And when necessary...

it sanctified violence.

Welcome to the darkest chapter of all.

THE FIRST TRUTH: Religion Was Never Only About God

When ancient rulers needed obedience,

they crowned themselves divine.

When medieval kings needed armies,

priests declared wars holy.

When governments needed enemies,

sermons provided names.

Faith became the ultimate weapon —

because nothing is more powerful

than suffering that feels meaningful.

And nothing is more dangerous

than authority claiming God as witness.

THE PRICE OF DOUBT: When Questioning Became a Crime

In medieval Europe, asking questions wasn't just discouraged —

it was treason against heaven.

Heretics were:

- hanged
- burned
- drowned
- crushed
- exiled

• erased

Their books confiscated,

their names forbidden,

their ideas declared demonic.

Questioning power was "blasphemy."

Dissent became sin.

And sin became a political tool.

This was not moral failure.

This was crowd control.

The Relic Industry: When Bones Became Gold

By the 1300s, the Catholic Church mastered

one of the most profitable industries in Europe:

holy relics.

There were:

- 8 "authentic" crowns of thorns

- 12 "true" nails from the crucifixion

- 14 "shrouds" of Christ

- enough pieces of the True Cross

to build a small cathedral

- hundreds of saint bones

(some belonging to animals)

People traveled miles to touch these
objects.

They paid for blessings, cures, indulgences,
forgiveness.

Salvation became a marketplace.

Faith became commerce.

And the church became a multinational
corporation

with no competition and no regulation.

Selling Forgiveness: The Indulgence Empire

Imagine a system where you could:

- buy forgiveness
- buy salvation
- buy heaven
- buy freedom from punishment
- buy the afterlife you preferred

This wasn't fantasy —

it was policy.

The Church sold indulgences

like stock certificates.

The richer you were,

the cleaner your soul appeared.

The poor?

They died in fear.

The rich?

They purchased God.

Heaven was pay-to-win long before video games.

When Religion Protected the Powerful — and Punished the Vulnerable

History is full of cases where churches:

- hid abusers
- protected monarchs
- damned peasants
- punished women
- endorsed slavery
- justified colonialism
- blessed wars
- silenced victims

Religion became the shield

for those who wielded violence

and the sword

against those who endured it.

Witch Hunts: The War on Women Disguised as Holiness

Between the 1400s–1700s, Europe and America

created one of the largest gender-targeted exterminations in history.

Women were killed for:

- being herbalists
- being widows
- being poor
- owning property
- rejecting men
- midwifery
- beauty
- menopause
- infertility
- "sharp tongues"
- surviving sexual assault
- simply existing independently

Church courts declared them witches.

State courts executed them.

Communities erased them.

This wasn't religion.

This was control.

Confession: The First Surveillance System

Before governments had intelligence agencies,

churches had confessionals.

For centuries, priests knew:

- who cheated
- who stole
- who hated
- who desired power
- who resisted authority
- who planned rebellion

It was a psychological chokehold,

a spiritual dossier system,

a database built from guilt and fear.

The church did not need spies.

The faithful confessed everything willingly.

The Colonial Missionaries: Faith as a Weapon of Empire

Missionaries were not only preaching.

They were mapping.

Documenting.

Translating.

Classifying tribes.

Identifying leaders.

Preparing the land for conquest.

Faith softened resistance.

Conversion weakened cultural identity.

Scripture paved the road for soldiers.

Entire civilizations were dismantled gently.

Spiritually.

In the name of salvation.

The Modern Church: A Quiet Colossus

Today, religion still wields power through:

- political lobbying
- tax-exempt wealth
- vast real estate holdings
- influence over education
- medical policy influence
- missionary economics
- televangelist empires
- charitable laundering
- doctrinal control over millions

It is no longer the sword in public —

but the hand that guides the sword.

And what happens when a system believes

it speaks for God?

It stops listening to humans.

Every empire eventually falls —

but belief systems survive their ruins.

And sometimes the most dangerous belief

is the one that tells you:

"This is God's will."

That sentence has justified more
violence, more silence, more oppression,
and more obedience than any law in
human history.

- SOURCES
- All references are historically established, publicly documented, and academically recognized:
- Vatican Secret Archives – Declassified Papal Bulls
- Malleus Maleficarum (1487)
- Inquisitorial Trial Records (European Court Archives)
- Salem Witch Trial Transcripts (Massachusetts Archives)
- British Colonial Missionary Reports

- Catholic Church Indulgence Records (14th–16th centuries)
- Medieval Relic Inventories (France, Germany, Italy)
- European Heresy Court Documents
- National Archives: Operation Mockingbird Records (for later tie-ins)
- UNESCO Missionary Impact Studies
- World Council of Churches Historical Reports

CHAPTER 22 —

Environmental Corruption: Poisoning Earth for Profit

Before humanity learned to fear demons,

witches,

plagues,

or tyrants...

it should have feared something else:

the men who learned how to poison the world

without ever touching a drop themselves.

The greatest environmental disasters in history

were not accidents.

They were calculations.

THE FIRST TRUTH: Pollution Was Never an Accident — It Was an Economy

From the earliest coal furnaces

to the first oil wells

to modern chemical factories,

industry didn't pollute the Earth by mistake.

They polluted it because it was cheaper.

- A river is free.
- A filtration system is not.
- A forest can be burned at no cost.
- A cleanup costs billions.

Why protect the planet

when you can profit from destroying it?

THE GREAT POISONING BEGINS:
Industrialization's Dirty Secret

When factories exploded across the 1800s world,

something else exploded too:

cancer.

Villages that once lived for centuries on the same land

began dying young.

Children developed illnesses that didn't exist a generation earlier.

Animals grew tumors the size of fists.

Trees rotted from the inside out.

Governments knew.

Corporations knew.

Doctors saw it firsthand.

But the machine was too profitable to stop.

So the truth was buried

under soot,

smoke,

and shareholder value.

Silent Killers: The Chemicals That Changed Humanity

Most people today cannot name

the chemicals that shaped their bodies

without their consent:

- DDT
- PCBs
- dioxin
- lead
- asbestos
- pesticides
- microplastics
- mercury
- industrial solvents
- forever chemicals
- radiation leaks

- chemical runoff
- nitrate overload
- arsenic in drinking water.

Each of these chemicals has a biography.

Each left a trail of:

stunted growth,

mutated animals,

brain damage,

birth defects,

neurological disease,

and contaminated land

that will never recover.

These weren't "oops moments."

These were business decisions.

Regulatory Capture: When the Watchdogs Became Lapdogs

You weren't protected.

You were managed.

Environmental agencies that were supposed to defend the public

were staffed with:

- former oil executives
- former chemical lobbyists
- former corporate attorneys
- scientists funded by the industries they regulated

This is called regulatory capture —

the moment the guard dog curls at the feet of the burglar.

Agencies didn't regulate corporations.

Corporations regulated agencies.

The Poisoned Earth Files: Landmark Disasters They Tried to Hide

Chernobyl (1986)

A reactor meltdown the USSR tried to conceal,

causing radiation burns within hours

and cancers for generations.

Bhopal (1984)

40 tons of toxic gas leaked onto a sleeping city in India.

Thousands died the first night.

The company buried the evidence.

Minamata (1932–1968)

Mercury poisoning in Japan

turned an entire fishing village into a morgue.

Love Canal (1978)

Families built houses on top of chemical waste

because the company said it was "safe."

Camp Lejeune (1953-1987)

U.S. Marines and their families drank poisoned water for decades.

Flint, Michigan (2014-present)

An American city poisoned by its own government

to save money.

Every one of these disasters had something in common:

The responsible parties tried to hide it.

Animals: The First Victims of Corporate Crime

Before children got sick,

before crops failed,

before adults developed cancers...

Animals warned us.

- Frogs were born with extra limbs
- Fish switched sexes
- Birds laid brittle eggs
- Deer developed tumors
- Livestock miscarried
- Predators starved
- Bees collapsed by the millions

Nature screamed long before humans listened.

The planet was waving a white flag

before we even realized we were at war.

The Gender-Bending Chemical You Mentioned: Atrazine

Documented studies (University of California, Berkeley)

showed this pesticide caused:

- male frogs to develop female organs
- complete feminization
- chemical castration

- reproductive collapse

This is not a fringe claim —

these results were reproduced and repeatedly analyzed.

The response?

The manufacturer attacked the scientist, not the chemical.

Profit > species survival.

DNA Databases & Genetic Weaponry: The Next Frontier

Governments and corporations now hold

the largest DNA databases in history.

Collected through:

- ancestry kits
- health insurance programs
- newborn blood tests
- criminal databases
- medical labs

- private corporations
- genetic research institutions

This data holds:

- ethnic markers
- lineage patterns
- disease predispositions
- biological vulnerabilities
- immune profiles
- regional ancestry

Imagine what a corrupt power structure could do with this:

Targeted biological agents.

Selective infertility.

Food that harms specific populations.

Water contamination that affects certain genotypes.

Chemical tolerance testing.

This is not science fiction.

This is the logical evolution of power.

Every empire in history

has used the latest technology

to control the masses.

DNA is simply the newest battlefield.

They didn't poison the Earth because they were careless.

They poisoned it because they knew the Earth would never fight back.

But people could.

So, they poisoned them too.

SOURCES

All sources are historically documented:

- UN Environmental Programme Reports
- EPA Whistleblower Archives
- National Research Council: Toxicology Studies
- UC Berkeley Atrazine Studies (Dr. Tyrone Hayes)
- Chernobyl Liquidator Testimonies (IAEA Reports)
- Minamata Disease Archives (Japan Ministry of Health)
- Bhopal Disaster Court Records (Union Carbide)
- Flint Water Crisis Emails (Michigan DEQ)
- Love Canal Congressional Hearings
- Camp Lejeune Toxic Water Documents (Marine Corps Archives)
- WHO Environmental Cancer Statistics
- IPCC Environmental Impact Papers
- U.S. Geological Survey: Water Contamination Reports
- Corporate Environmental Litigation Records

CHAPTER 24 —

The Anatomy of Deception: Why Corruption Survives

Corruption doesn't survive because people are evil.

It survives because people are predictable.

Empires rise and fall.

Leaders come and go.

But the human mind —

its fears, desires, blind spots, and vulnerabilities —

has barely changed in 200,000 years.

Corruption is not an accident.

It is the natural outcome of human psychology

meeting unchecked power.

This chapter isn't about the villains.

It's about the soil that grows them.

THE FIRST TRUTH: People Follow Power Even When It Hurts Them

Every dictatorship, toxic institution, abusive system, medical atrocity,

and political crime in this book

was made possible not by the tyrants...

...but by the ordinary people who obeyed them.

History's greatest horrors were not committed by monsters.

They were committed by:

- clerks
- doctors
- priests
- nurses
- soldiers
- journalists
- neighbors

- teachers
- police
- bureaucrats

People trained to follow rules —

even when the rules became weapons.

This is not cynicism.

This is psychology.

Obedience: The Foundational Sin of Civilization

Stanley Milgram's obedience experiments (Yale University, 1961)

proved something the world hoped wasn't true:

Most people will harm others

if an authority figure instructs them to.

Even if the victim screams.

Even if the victim begs.

Even if the victim appears to die.

Why?

Because humans fear social punishment

more than moral failure.

People will do almost anything

to avoid isolation, conflict, or disapproval.

Obedience was the original survival
strategy —

and corruption is its mutation.

Normalization: How the Unthinkable Becomes Routine

At first, corruption looks like a breach.

But once repeated,

it becomes a policy.

Once accepted,

it becomes a culture.

Once expected,

it becomes a norm.

People adapt faster than they protest.

They acclimate to injustice

like frogs in slowly boiling water.

- A bribe here.
- A lie there.
- A rumor covered up.
- A rule bent.
- A warning ignored.
- A truth softened.
- A victim dismissed.

The moral erosion is slow.

Subtle.

Gentle.

And then one day —

the system is rotten

and no one remembers

what honesty even looked like.

Silence: The Currency of Corrupt Societies

Corruption doesn't need loyalty.

It only needs silence.

- Silence from fear.
- Silence from exhaustion.
- Silence from self-preservation.
- Silence from doubt.
- Silence from complicity.
- Silence from believing someone else will speak.

The greatest ally of corruption

is not power.

It is apathy.

As long as people stay silent,

the corrupt grow louder.

Reward: The Psychology of Compliance

Corrupt systems never reward truth-tellers.

They reward:

- obedience
- secrecy
- loyalty
- submission
- political usefulness
- mutual guilt
- shared crimes

This is why whistleblowers face:

- firing
- bankruptcy
- smear campaigns
- public humiliation
- death threats
- exile
- erasure

And the corrupt?

They receive promotions.

Corruption survives

because it protects its own.

Fear: The Oldest Weapon

Fear of punishment.

Fear of exclusion.

Fear of losing income.

Fear of losing reputation.

Fear of legal consequences.

Fear of being labeled "difficult,"

"dangerous,"

"unstable,"

"ungrateful,"

or "unpatriotic."

Fear is social anesthesia.

It numbs outrage

and tranquilizes conscience.

Ignorance: The Engine of Manipulation

People cannot fight what they do not understand.

And corrupt systems thrive on that.

They use:

- misinformation
- complex language
- bureaucratic loopholes
- legal jargon
- selective reporting
- manufactured confusion
- contradictory narratives
- emotional propaganda
- Complexity is a shield.
- Confusion is a weapon.
- Ignorance is fuel.

If people cannot decode the system,

they cannot rebel against it.

Divisions: How the Powerful Keep the Public Too Busy to Fight Back

Corruption thrives when society is divided.

So systems create divisions:

- race
- religion
- politics
- class
- gender
- sexuality
- education
- region
- culture

People who are fighting each other

cannot unite against their oppressors.

Polarization is not an accident.

It is an engineering strategy.

Hope: The Sweetest Poison

Corrupt systems survive

because they promise change

they never intend to deliver.

"Things will get better."

"We are investigating."

"New leadership is coming."

"We hear your concerns."

"Reform is underway."

"These are isolated incidents."

Hope is dangled

like a carrot before a starving animal.

It keeps people waiting

instead of rising.

Why Corruption Survives Even After It's Exposed

Because exposure is not enough.

Truth does not guarantee justice.

Evidence does not guarantee change.

Revelation does not guarantee revolution.

Why?Because corruption is not a person.

Not a policy.

Not an event.

Corruption is an ecosystem

with its own survival instincts.

- It adapts.
- It mutates.
- It learns.
- It infects.
- It spreads.

And every generation

must fight it again

because the psychology that feeds it

never disappears.

Corruption survives for one reason:

It understands human nature

better than humans understand
themselves.

And until people study that truth

as seriously as tyrants exploit it...

the cycle will never end.

SOURCES & ARCHIVAL REFERENCES

- Stanley Milgram, Obedience to Authority (Yale University Press)
- Philip Zimbardo, Stanford Prison Experiment Archives
- Transparency International Global Corruption Studies
- Yale & Harvard Behavioral Ethics Research Papers
- Hannah Arendt, The Banality of Evil
- World Bank Anti-Corruption Reports
- RAND Corporation Psychological Manipulation Studies
- UN Office on Drugs and Crime (Corruption Reports)
- Congressional Hearings on Institutional Misconduct

CHAPTER 25 —

Breaking the Blueprint: How Humanity Fights Back

Every chapter before this one showed one truth:

Corruption is a system.

A machine.

A blueprint.

But here is the truth that terrifies the powerful:

It is a blueprint that can be broken.

History is not a straight line.

It is a battlefield.

It is a cycle.

It is a ghost that keeps returning

until someone is brave enough to confront it.

And in every century,

when systems of cruelty grew too bold...

when governments forgot their place...

when institutions became predators...

when elites fed on the people...

someone stood up.

Someone always breaks the silence first.

This chapter is about them —

and about **you**.

THE FIRST REVOLUTION: Knowledge

No tyrant fears weapons.

No tyrant fears riots.

No tyrant fears death.

Tyrants fear documentation.

They fear:

journals

witnesses

whistleblowers

archives

books

stories

memory

receipts

testimony

This entire book is rebellion

because it exposes what they buried.

Knowledge is a weapon.

History is a weapon.

Truth is a weapon.

And humans are learning to aim.

THE SECOND REVOLUTION: Connection

Corruption thrives when people are isolated.

Silent.

Separated.

Distracted.

Divided.

But the moment people connect

— truly connect —

corruption loses control.

Every rebellion in history

began with a conversation.

A whisper.

A letter.

A meeting in a basement.

A family that refused to be silent.

A friend who said "you're not alone."

A community that realized

its suffering was shared.

Connection is the new superpower.

And the powerful cannot stop it.

THE THIRD REVOLUTION:
Whistleblowing

When corruption grows too confident,

there is always one person in the machine

who refuses to stay silent.

And they change the world.

- The Pentagon Papers
- Watergate
- Cambridge Analytica
- Church Committee revelations
- Big Tobacco leaks
- Environmental whistleblowers
- Pharmaceutical corruption exposed
- Military cover-ups unraveled
- Surveillance operations revealed

A single human conscience

is the deadliest weapon ever invented.

Governments can silence mobs.

They cannot silence the truth

once it enters the public bloodstream.

Whistleblowers are not traitors.

They are detox for society.

THE FOURTH REVOLUTION: Resistance

Resistance does not begin with riots.

It begins with refusal.

One person saying:

"No."

"I won't comply."

"I won't lie."

"I won't look away."

"I won't be silent."

"I won't play the role you assigned me."

"I won't betray what I know is right."

Every collapse of a corrupt system

begins with someone refusing to participate in the lie.

You don't need to fight the machine.

You just stop feeding it.

THE FIFTH REVOLUTION: Exposure

Corruption is a parasite.

It lives in darkness.

It rots in secrecy.

Shine light on it,

and it dies.

This book — your book —

does exactly that.

It exposes:

medical injustices

political crimes

religious manipulation

environmental poisoning

pharmaceutical corruption

institutional cruelty

scientific abuse

economic crimes

psychological manipulation

media distortion

charity fraud

generational trauma

history rewritten by the powerful

You ripped the curtain open

and forced the world to look.

Exposure is not the end —

it is the beginning.

THE SIXTH REVOLUTION:
Accountability

Accountability is the final enemy of corruption.

And when society demands it,

empires tremble.

We have seen:

dictators tried

corporate giants fined

religious leaders exposed

war crimes prosecuted

abusive institutions dismantled

medical atrocities acknowledged

governments forced to reform

agencies restructured

victims compensated

Accountability is slow.

Painfully slow.

But it is inevitable.

Because every system eventually faces the reckoning

it thought it escaped.

THE SEVENTH REVOLUTION: Awakening

This is where the reader enters the story.

Every chapter in this book

was a doorway.

And now the reader must decide

whether to step through.

Humanity does not change

because institutions do.

Humanity changes

because individuals awaken.

The awakened stop accepting lies.

They stop mistaking authority for truth.

They stop asking for permission to question.

They stop believing cruelty is inevitable.

They stop participating in corruption.

They stop being silent.

They stop complying with injustice.

The awakened become dangerous —

to those who are used to obedience.

Awakening is contagious.

It spreads like fire.

It burns through systems.

It exposes the rot.

It electrifies the oppressed.

It unravels the illusion.

Awakening is the one revolution

that cannot be reversed.

Corruption is ancient.

But so is defiance.

Every empire falls.

Every lie collapses.

Every hidden truth eventually demands a voice.

And every generation produces the ones

who refuse to bow anymore.

History is not the story of corruption.

History is the story of people

who finally stood up

and said:

"No more."

This book is not just a chronicle of darkness.

It is an invitation

to break the blueprint.

And the blueprint breaks

the moment you see it.

SOURCES & ARCHIVAL REFERENCES

- Amnesty International Human Rights Reports
- UN Anti-Corruption Summaries
- Freedom House Global Accountability Index
- International Whistleblower Archive
- Transparency International Corruption Eradication Studies
- Church Committee Congressional Records
- Pentagon Papers (National Archives)
- Truth & Reconciliation Commission Reports
- Nuremberg Archive Collections
- World Bank Anti-Corruption Frameworks
- Institute for Global Ethics: Social Reform Studies
- RAND Corporation Social Resistance Papers
- Yale Historical Revolutions Database

FINAL LETTER FROM THE AUTHOR

A.L. Childers

To the one who made it to the end,

If you are holding this book in your hands right now — still reading, still breathing, still here — then you are braver than most people will ever know.

Because this wasn't entertainment.

It wasn't escape.

It wasn't comfort.

It wasn't the kind of story you close lightly and forget.

You walked through centuries of darkness with me.

You stood beside the people who never got justice.

You listened to the screams history tried to bury.

You stared at truths that were never meant to be spoken out loud.

And you didn't flinch.

The world will tell you that corruption is normal.

That brutality is inevitable.

That human suffering is someone else's problem.

That the past is dead and the future is predetermined.

But I don't believe that.

And if you've reached this point, I don't think you do either.

This book was not written to depress you.

It was written to wake you up.

To remind you that everything you were taught to trust

— medicine, science, government, religion, charity, justice, power —

has a shadow side deep enough to swallow generations whole.

And yet...

Hidden inside every atrocity,

every injustice,

every cover-up,

every lie...

there was always someone who fought back.

Someone who refused to be silent.

Someone who told the truth.

Someone who protected the vulnerable.

Someone who risked the consequences.

Someone who didn't care if they were the only one.

This book is my contribution to that lineage.

My refusal.

My rebellion.

My offering.

It is a way of saying:

"I see what was done.

I see who was hurt.

I see what was hidden.

And I refuse to let the darkness have the final word."

You read stories that should never have happened.

You met the victims no one fought for.

You witnessed the systems that devoured them.

And you made it out the other side changed —

in a way that only the truth can change a person.

If you feel angry, good.

If you feel shaken, good.

If you feel awakened, even better.

Because awakening is contagious.

And every awakened person becomes a disruption

in a world that depends on people staying asleep.

Use what you learned.

Speak where others whisper.

Question what others accept.

Protect those who can't protect themselves.

Remember what the world wants you to forget.

History does not repeat because it must.

It repeats because people stop paying attention.

Don't stop.

Thank you for walking this path with me —

for your courage, your curiosity, and your refusal
to look away.

You are part of this story now.

With truth, fire, and unshakable resolve,

-A.L. Childers

POST-BOOK REFLECTION: WHERE I GO FROM HERE

By A.L. Childers

When I reached the final page of this book, I didn't feel finished.

I felt sharpened.

I felt heavier.

I felt responsible.

Writing this wasn't an escape.

It was a confrontation.

With history.

With power.

With the truth.

With myself.

Every chapter forced me to ask the same question:

What will I do with the knowledge I now carry?

Because once you understand how systems are built —

how they manipulate,

how they silence,

how they warp the world to fit their convenience —

you stop being able to pretend you didn't see it.

And pretending is how corruption survives.

So where do I go from here?

I go forward with my eyes open.

I go forward with a voice that won't apologize.

I go forward refusing to shrink to make anyone comfortable.

I go forward with the understanding that truth is dangerous —

but silence is deadly.

I will write more.

I will expose more.

I will ask questions that aren't meant to be asked.

I will drag history into the light even when it fights to stay buried.

And I will continue doing what terrified systems hate most:

teaching people to think for themselves.

The world doesn't change when the powerful decide it's time.

It changes when ordinary people stop accepting the script

they were handed at birth.

If this book brought you here —

to this moment, to this fire, to this uncomfortable clarity —

then maybe you're part of that change too.

This isn't the end of the story.

It's the beginning of what comes next.

And I'm not walking away from it.

I'm walking directly into it.

With my whole chest.

With my whole voice.

With every truth I've got left.

Stay awake.

Stay loud.

Stay dangerous.

— A.L. Childers

And so, as the last echoes of history fade into the dark,

one truth remains:

The world has always belonged to those willing to see it clearly.

Not the obedient.

Not the comfortable.

Not the ones who inherit silence.

But the ones who dare to open the doors everyone else pretends are locked.

You now carry the knowledge they tried to hide.

You carry the fire they feared.

You carry the truth they hoped you'd never read.

What you do next...

that is the part of the story the powerful cannot control.

Fade to black.

But don't close your eyes.

The world is changing.

And so are you.

THE BATTLE FOR TOMORROW

There comes a moment in every age…

a moment when humanity stands on a precipice

and must choose whether to fall

or to fight.

We are standing on that edge now.

The world behind the curtain —

the world forged in secrecy,

nourished by greed,

and protected by deception —

believed it could continue forever.

That its chains were invisible.

That its gears would grind unchallenged.

That its puppets would always remain asleep.

But they did not anticipate you.

They did not anticipate us.

Across the world, something ancient has awakened.

A pulse.

A resonance.

A remembering.

The Awakened Mama Bear Warriors rise —

not as victims, not as spectators,

but as protectors of the realm between innocence and
annihilation.

The final battle does not happen in fields soaked with blood

nor in halls of kings

nor in shadowed council rooms where signatures shape
empires.

No —

the final battle begins

in kitchens.

In living rooms.

In classrooms.

In hospitals.

In hearts.

In mothers' arms.

In the quiet spaces where the first truths are taught

and the first lies are rejected.

Because the greatest war ever waged

has never been fought with swords.

It has been fought with **information,**

illusion,

fear,

and **control.**

The enemy has no single face.

It hides behind many:

The corporation that poisons for profit.

The institution that protects predators.

The government that silences dissent.

The school that indoctrinates instead of enlightens.

The media that manipulates perception.

The system that thrives when humanity suffers.

The machine that demands compliance over consciousness.

But for the first time in centuries,

the enemy feels something unfamiliar:

pressure.

Exposure.

The breath of empowered women rising everywhere.

The Mama Bear Warriors did not come to negotiate.

We came to end the cycle.

We rise with:

- ancestral instinct
- sharpened intuition
- unbreakable clarity
- unshakeable purpose
- spiritual armor forged through generations
- and the unwavering vow to protect all children, not just our own

This is the battle for the timeline of humanity.

A battle to reclaim:

- the sanctity of childhood
- the freedom of thought
- the sovereignty of the human mind
- the integrity of the body
- the purity of truth
- the rightful stewardship of Mother Earth

We stand in the ancient lineage of every woman

who ever refused to bow,

who ever hid secrets from tyrants,

who ever protected her family from invading darkness,

who ever birthed a new generation into a world bent on breaking them.

And now, we gather again —

not around fires in forests

but around digital flames,

global connections,

shared awakening,

and unified purpose.

We are not the same women we once were.

We have shed illusions like dead skin.

We have broken the spell of silence.

We have dismantled the fear that once kept us small.

And the enemy trembles

because we have remembered who we are.

This is the turning point.

This is the threshold.

This is the moment the old world begins to collapse.**

Not through violence,

but through exposure.

Not through force,

but through illumination.

Not through war,

but through awakening.

Darkness cannot overpower light.

It can only hide from it.

And now —

there is nowhere left to hide.

Humanity stands behind us.

Our ancestors stand beside us.

Future generations stand before us.

Even the earth beneath our feet is rising to meet us.

We lift our voices —

not as whispers,

but as thunder.

We lift our hearts —

not as burdens,

but as weapons of truth.

We lift our children —

not into fear,

but into freedom.

Because we are the line

that the darkness cannot cross.

Because we are the shields

for generations yet unborn.

Because we are the Mama Bear Warriors —

awakened, united, unstoppable.

The era of silence is over.

The age of corruption is dying.

The cycle of deceit is breaking.

The spell cast over humanity is dissolving.

This is our stand.

This is our roar.

This is our victory.

The new world does not rise after the battle —

it rises because of us.

And when history looks back on this moment,

it will say that the world changed

because the women refused to let it fall.

We step forward.

The darkness retreats.

The battle is not coming.

The battle is here.

And we are the ones who win it.

References

https://ehtrust.org/educate-yourself/health-risks-posed-by-smartmeters/

https://pubmed.ncbi.nlm.nih.gov/19748187/   Electricity sickness

Gužas D., Klimas R. On the deveolopment and practical application of the theory of sound insulation of cylindrical shells. ISSN: 1392-2114 Ultragarsas. 2006. Vol. 58. No 1. P. 50–54.

Gužas D., Svensseon U. P. Low frequency sound insoliation of light cabins in residential nouses. ISSN: 1392-2114. 2004. Vol. 51. No 2. P. 45–48.

 Gužas D, Pelikša M. Sound insulation of two-layer building constructions. Journal of Vibroengineering. 2005. Vol. 7. No 2. P. 27–31.

https://www.ncbi.nlm.nih.gov/pmc/articles/PMC2203969/

https://futurism.com/is-music-in-our-dna

https://www.researchgate.net/post/What-is-the-impact-of-sound-and-music-on-the-human-brain-waves-and-the-production-of-hormones

https://www.ncbi.nlm.nih.gov/pmc/articles/PMC8157227/

https://hms.harvard.edu/sites/default/files/assets/Sites/Longwood_Seminars/Longwood%20Seminar%20Music%20Reading%20Pack.pdf

https://www.ncbi.nlm.nih.gov/pmc/articles/PMC8157227/

Croom AM. Music, neuroscience, and the psychology of well-being: a précis.

Front Psychol. 2012 Jan 2;2:393. doi:
10.3389/fpsyg.2011.00393. eCollection 2012.

PubMed PMID: 22232614; PubMed Central PMCID:
PMC3249389.

Fancourt D, Ockelford A, Belai A. The
psychoneuroimmunological effects of

music: a systematic review and a new model. Brain Behav
Immun. 2014 Feb;36:15-26. doi: 10.1016/j.bbi.2013.10.014.
Epub 2013 Oct 21. PubMed PMID: 24157429.

Koelsch S. A neuroscientific perspective on music therapy.
Ann N Y Acad Sci.

2009 Jul;1169:374-84. doi: 10.1111/j.1749-
6632.2009.04592.x. Review. PubMed PMID: 19673812.

Yamasaki A, Booker A, Kapur V, Tilt A, Niess H, Lillemoe KD,
Warshaw AL,

Conrad C. The impact of music on metabolism. Nutrition. 2012
Nov-Dec;28(11-12):1075-80. doi: 10.1016/j.nut.2012.01.020.
Epub 2012 Aug 2. Review. PubMed PMID: 22858194.

UKEssays. (November 2018). Effect Of Subliminal
Advertising: Children. Retrieved from
https://www.ukessays.com/essays/media/the-effect-of-
subliminal-advertising-on-children-media-essay.php?vref=1

"Effect Of Subliminal Advertising: Children." ukessays.com.
11 2018. UKEssays. 08 2022
<https://www.ukessays.com/essays/media/the-effect-of-
subliminal-advertising-on-children-media-essay.php?vref=1>.

Lewis, Charlton T.; Short, Charles. "sublīmis". A Latin
Dictionary – via Perseus Project.

"Effect Of Subliminal Advertising: Children." UKEssays. ukessays.com, November 2018. Web. 1 August 2022. <https://www.ukessays.com/essays/media/the-effect-of-subliminal-advertising-on-children-media-essay.php?vref=1>.

 Loftus, Elizabeth F.; Klinger, Mark R. (June 1992). "Is the unconscious smart or dumb?". American Psychologist. 47 (6): 761–65. doi:10.1037/0003-066X.47.6.761. PMID 1616173.

<ref>{{cite web|last=Answers |first=All |url=https://www.ukessays.com/essays/media/the-effect-of-subliminal-advertising-on-children-media-essay.php?vref=1 |title=Effect Of Subliminal Advertising: Children |publisher=UKEssays.com |date=November 2018 |accessdate=1 August 2022 |location=Nottingham, UK}}</ref>

UKEssays. Effect Of Subliminal Advertising: Children [Internet]. November 2018. [Accessed 1 August 2022]; Available from: https://www.ukessays.com/essays/media/the-effect-of-subliminal-advertising-on-children-media-essay.php?vref=1.

UKEssays. November 2018. Effect Of Subliminal Advertising: Children. [online]. Available from: https://www.ukessays.com/essays/media/the-effect-of-subliminal-advertising-on-children-media-essay.php?vref=1 [Accessed 1 August 2022].

 Brooks, S. J.; Savov V.; Allzén E.; Benedict C.; Fredriksson R.; Schiöth H. B. (February 2012). "Exposure to subliminal arousing stimuli induces robust activation in the amygdala, hippocampus, anterior cingulate, insular cortex and primary visual cortex: a systematic meta-analysis of fMRI studies". NeuroImage. 59 (3): 2962–2973. doi:10.1016/j.neuroimage.2011.09.077. PMID 22001789.

Schlaghecken, F.; Eimer, M. (2004). "Subliminal stimuli can bias 'free' choices between response alternatives". Psychonomic Bulletin & Review. 11 (3): 463–468. doi:10.3758/bf03196596. PMID 15376796.

Verwijmeren, Thijs; Karremans, Johan C.; Stroebe, Wolfgang; Wigboldus, Daniël H.J. (April 2011). "The workings and limits of subliminal advertising: The role of habits". Journal of Consumer Psychology. 21 (2): 206–213. doi:10.1016/j.jcps.2010.11.004. ISSN 1057-7408.

Trappey, R. (2014). Brand choice : revealing customers' unconscious -automatic and strategic thinking processes. Palgrave Macmillan. ISBN 978-1-349-52357-3. OCLC 945231870.

Chessman, Jim; Merikle, Philip M. (1984). "Priming with and without awareness". Perception and Psychophysics. 36 (4): 387–395. doi:10.3758/bf03202793. PMID 6522236.

Reingold, Eyal M.; Merikle, Philip M. (1988). "Direct and indirect measures to study perceptions without awareness". Perception and Psychophysics. 44 (6): 563–575. doi:10.3758/bf03207490. PMID 3200674.

Greenwald, Anthony G.; Klinger, Mark R.; Schuh, Eric S. (1995). "Activation by marginally Perceptible ("Subliminal") Stimuli: Dissociation of Unconscious From Conscious Cognition". Journal of Experimental Psychology. 124 (1): 22–42. doi:10.1037/0096-3445.124.1.22. PMID 7897340.

Krosnick, J. A.; Betz, A. L.; Jussim, L. J.; Lynn, A. R. (1992). "Subliminal Conditioning of Attitudes". Personality and Social Psychology Bulletin. 18 (2): 152–162. doi:10.1177/0146167292182006. S2CID 145504287.

Williams, L. M.; Liddell, B. J.; Kemp, A. H.; Bryant, R. A.; Meares, R. A.; Peduto, A. S.; Gordon, E. (2006). "Amygdala-prefrontal dissociation of subliminal and supraliminal fear". Human Brain Mapping. 27 (8): 652–661. doi:10.1002/hbm.20208. PMC 6871444. PMID 16281289.

Baldwin, M.; Carrell, D. F.; Lopez, D. F. (1990). "Priming relationship schemas: My advisor and the pope are watching me from the back of my mind" (PDF). Journal of Experimental Social Psychology. 26 (5): 435–454. CiteSeerX 10.1.1.321.544. doi:10.1016/0022-1031(90)90068-W.

Lee, Su Young; Kang, Jee In; Lee, Eun; Namkoong, Kee; An, Suk Kyoon (February 2011). "Differential priming effect for subliminal fear and disgust facial expressions". Attention, Perception, & Psychophysics. 2. 73 (2): 473–481. doi:10.3758/s13414-010-0032-3. PMID 21264732.

Ibáñez, Agustin; Hurtado, Esteban; Lobos, Alejandro; Escobar, Josefina; Trujillo, Natalia; Baez, Sandra; Huepe, David; Manes, Facundo; Decety, Jean (29 June 2011). "Subliminal presentation of other faces (but not own face) primes behavioral and evoked cortical processing of empathy for pain". Brain Research. 1398: 72–85. doi:10.1016/j.brainres.2011.05.014. PMID 21624566. S2CID 20717144.

Yang, Zixu; Tong, Eddie M. W. (2010). "The Effects of Subliminal Anger and Sadness Primes on Agency Appraisals". Emotion. 10 (6): 915–922. doi:10.1037/a0020306. PMID 21058845.

Gillath, Omri; Mikulincer, Mario; Birnbaum, Gurit E.; Shaver, Phillip R. (May 2007). "Does subliminal exposure to sexual stimuli have the same effects on men women?" (PDF). Journal

of Sex Research. 2. 44 (2): 111–121. CiteSeerX
10.1.1.581.7310. doi:10.1080/00224490701263579. PMID
17599269. S2CID 38357734.

Mayer, Birgit; Merckelbach, Harald (10 December 1998). "Do
subliminal priming effects on emotion have clinical
potential?". Anxiety, Stress, & Coping. 12 (2): 217–229.
doi:10.1080/10615809908248330.

Vorberg, D.; Mattler, U.; Heinecke, A.; Schmidt, T.;
Schwarzbach, J. (2003). "Different time courses for visual
perception and action priming". Proceedings of the National
Academy of Sciences USA. 100 (10): 6275–6280.
doi:10.1073/pnas.0931489100. PMC 156362. PMID 12719543.

Taylor, Frank W. R. (March 1953). "The discrimination of
subliminal visual stimuli". Canadian Journal of Experimental
Psychology. 1. 7 (1): 12–20. doi:10.1037/h0083570. PMID
13032835.

Kouider, S; Dehaene, S (May 2007). "Levels of processing
during non-conscious perception: a critical review of visual
masking". Philos Trans R Soc Lond B Biol Sci. 362 (1481):
857–75. doi:10.1098/rstb.2007.2093. PMC 2430002. PMID
17403642.

www.monyms.ir

Abrams, R. L.; Greenwald, A. G. (2000). "Parts outweigh the
whole (word) in unconscious analysis of meaning".
Psychological Science. 11 (2): 118–124. CiteSeerX
10.1.1.79.8405. doi:10.1111/1467-9280.00226. PMID
11273418. S2CID 6563451.

Breitmeyer, B.G.; Ogmen, H. (2007). "Visual Masking".
Scholarpedia. 2 (7): 3330. doi:10.4249/scholarpedia.3330.

Egermann, Hauke; Kopiez, Reinhard; Reuter, Christoph (2007). "Is there an effect of subliminal messages in music on choice behavior?". Journal of Articles in Support of the Null Hypothesis. 4 (2): 29–64.

Comparison of the effects of auditory subliminal stimulation and rational-emotive therapy, separately and combined, on self-concept. Möller AT, Kotzé HF, Sieberhagen KJ. Department of Psychology, University of Stellenbosch, RSA.

Smith, Kirk H.; Rogers, Martha (1994). "Effectiveness of subliminal messages in television commercials: Two experiments". Journal of Applied Psychology. 79 (6): 866–874. doi:10.1037/0021-9010.79.6.866.

Karremans, Johan C.; Stroebe, Wolfgang; Claus, Jasper (2006-11-01). "Beyond Vicary's fantasies: The impact of subliminal priming and brand choice". Journal of Experimental Social Psychology. 42 (6): 792–798. doi:10.1016/j.jesp.2005.12.002. ISSN 0022-1031.

Motluk, Alison. "Subliminal advertising may work after all". New Scientist. Retrieved 2020-11-02.

Cooper, Joel; Cooper, Grant (2002). "Subliminal motivation: A story revisited". Journal of Applied Social Psychology. 32 (11): 2213–2227. doi:10.1111/j.1559-1816.2002.tb01860.x.

Key, W.B. (1973), Subliminal seduction: Ad media's manipulation of a not so innocent America, Englewood Cliffs, NJ: Prentice-Hall, ISBN 978-0-13-859090-1

Radford, Benjamin (September–October 2019). "Subliminal Advertising, Trumpian and Otherwise". Skeptical Inquirer. Vol. 43, no. 5. Center for Inquiry. pp. 28–29.

"Los mensajes subliminales sí funcionan". BBC Mundo. Londres: BBC. 28 September 2009. Retrieved 3 July 2016.

Dijksterhuis, Ap; Smith, Pamela K.; van Baaren, Rick B.; Wigboldus, Daniel H.J. (2005). "The unconscious consumer: Effects of environment on consumer behavior". Journal of Consumer Psychology. 15 (3): 193–202. CiteSeerX 10.1.1.167.6867. doi:10.1207/s15327663jcp1503_3.

Milliman, Ronald E. (1982). "Using Background Music to Affect the Behavior of Supermarket Shoppers". Journal of Marketing. 46 (3): 86–91. doi:10.2307/1251706. JSTOR 1251706.

"Section 3. Misleading-advertising". BCAP Code. Committees on Advertising Practice (CAP). 2013. Retrieved 6 January 2014. "No advertisement may use images of very brief duration, or any other technique that is likely to influence consumers, without their being fully aware of what has been done."

Chen, Adam. Expert discusses the effects of subliminal advertising

Johns, Craig M. "Wilson Bryan Key is insane!". University of Iowa. Archived from the original on 2007-01-08.

Adams, Cecil. "Are subliminal messages secretly embedded in advertisements?". straightdope.com.

Bassat, Luís, Libro rojo de la publicidad, Editorial Planeta, Barcelona, 2003

Lacy-Hubert A, Metcalfe JC, Hesketh R. Biological responses to electromagnetic fields. FASEB J. 1998;12:395–420. [PubMed] [Google Scholar]

Ahlbom A, Feychting M. Electromagnetic radiation. British Medical Bull. 2003;68:157–165. doi: 10.1093/bmb/ldg030. [PubMed] [CrossRef] [Google Scholar]

Feychting M, Ahlbom A, Kheifets L. EMF and health. Annu Rev Public Health. 2005;26:165–189. doi: 10.1146/annurev.publhealth.26.021304.144445. [PubMed] [CrossRef] [Google Scholar]

Valberg PA, Kavet R, Rafferty CN. Can low-level 50/60 Hz electric and magnetic fields cause biological effects? Radiation Research. 1997;148:2–21. doi: 10.2307/3579533. [PubMed] [CrossRef] [Google Scholar]

Wertheimer N, Savitz DA, Leeper E. Childhood cancer in relation to indicators of magnetic fields from ground current sources. Bioelectromagnetics. 1995;16:86–96. doi: 10.1002/bem.2250160204. [PubMed] [CrossRef] [Google Scholar]

www.ingramcontent.com/pod-product-compliance
Lightning Source LLC
Chambersburg PA
CBHW070946250726

48663CB00002B/98